The Book of Jeremiah
and
Lamentations
God Has Spoken
A Commentary and Questions

Lucian Farrar, Jr.

James Kay Publishing

Tulsa, Oklahoma

The Book of Jeremiah and Lamentations
God Has Spoken
ISBN 978-1-943245-77-2

www.jameskaypublishing.com

e-mail: sales@jameskaypublishing.com

Other Books by Lucian Farrar, Jr.

The Book of Daniel
The Most High Rules
A Commentary and Questions

The Victorious Church
In the Book of Revelation
A Commentary and Questions

The Minor Prophets
God's Spokesmen
A Commentary and Questions

The Book of Isaiah
Christ, Our Redeemer
A Commentary and Questions

The Life of Christ
A Chronological Account

Psalms
Book 1
David's Original Collection

Psalms
Books 2 & 3

The King and His Kingdom in Acts

Scriptures are from the Kings James Version
with archaic words, forms, and punctuations
replaced by those in current use.

Other translations are acknowledged
by the following abbreviations:

ESV – English Standard Version

NASB – New American Standard Bible

NIV – New International Version

NKJV – New King James Version

Dedication

This book is dedicated to all who are preaching and teaching the word of God. Jeremiah sets a good example as God's spokesman to a sinful and rebellious people. At times you will get discouraged as Jeremiah did. Return to God, your source of strength and authority, and continue to preach and teach God's word as Jeremiah did.

— Lucian Farrar, Jr.

Thank you,
> To Bob Colvin for proofreading this book.

Table of Contents

Contents

Lesson 1

The Book of Jeremiah

God Has Spoken

When the LORD descended upon Mount Sinai, he spoke all the words of the Ten Commandments with his own voice. (Exodus 19:18; 20:1-19) He also spoke through his prophets. In the New Testament we read: "No prophecy was ever made by the act of human will, but men moved by the Holy Spirit spoke from God." (2 Peter 1:21) [NASB]

Jeremiah proclaims that he is speaking the word of the LORD. More than one-hundred-fifty times in his prophecy, he says, "The word of the LORD came." [1] Also, he uses other phrases such as: "But the LORD said to me," and "thus says the LORD." Jeremiah states 483 times that he is speaking the words of the LORD. [2] God has spoken! He must be heard, respected, and obeyed.

The Historical Setting

Jeremiah began his work *in the days of Josiah king of Judah, in the thirteenth year of his reign.* **1:2** The year was 626 BC. These were troublesome times. The kingdom of Israel had been destroyed by the Assyrians ninety-five years earlier. But the southern kingdom of Judah had been spared by the faithfulness of King Hezekiah, the great grandfather of Josiah.[3] However, Josiah's grandfather Manasseh and his father Amon had led the nation of Judah into idolatry. Because of their wickedness, God had decided to destroy the city of

---

[1] Wayne Jackson, *Jeremiah & Lamentations*, p. 4
[2] Robert Taylor, Jr., *Studies in Jeremiah, Volume One*, p. 1
[3] 2 Kings 18 - 19

Jerusalem and to deliver the kingdom of Judah "into the hand of their enemies." [4]

Josiah was the last good king of Judah. He began purging the land of idolatry when he was twenty years old. Six years later, he ordered the temple to be repaired so that the true worship of the LORD could be restored, including the observance of the Passover. [5]

Warren Wiersbe observes, "Unfortunately, the obedience of many of the people was only a surface thing. Unlike the king, they displayed no true repentance. It was reformation instead of repentance." [6] Jeremiah told his people that the LORD had said, ***"Judah has not returned to Me with her whole heart, but in pretense."*** **Jer. 3:10** [NKJV] When Josiah was killed in battle at the young age of 39, the nation returned to idolatry and wickedness. [7]

In the thirteenth year of Josiah's reign, Jeremiah urged his people to repent of their sinful ways and return to the LORD in humble obedience. (7:2-7) Jeremiah had an active role in King Josiah's reformation movement. But after Josiah's death, the nation returned to idolatry during the reigns of the last three kings of Judah. Jeremiah had to warn them of the coming destruction of Jerusalem and their exile in Babylon.

Jeremiah the Man

Jeremiah is often called "The Weeping Prophet" because of his Lamentations over the destroyed city of Jerusalem. But a more fitting description of Jeremiah would be **"The Prophet of Terror, Tears and Triumph."** He spoke words of **terror** about their impending doom. He had **tears** for the sufferings of his people and for the destruction of Jerusalem and the

---

[4] 2 Kings 21:10-15
[5] 2 Chronicles 34:5 – 35:19
[6] Warren W. Wiersbe, *Be Decisive,* p. 14
[7] 2 Kings 23:28-37

temple. However, he was a prophet of **triumph** with a message of future hope. He promised the return of the Jews from exile and the coming of Christ with his new covenant, in which their sins would be remembered no more.

Jeremiah was the only Old Testament prophet who was instructed not to marry. (See 16:1-2.) This would symbolize the loss of family members during the coming days. Also, Jeremiah needed to be totally devoted to his prophetic work during these turbulent times. (1 Cor. 7:26-35.)

Jeremiah would be considered a failure by human standards. He preached for more than forty years, and very few people listened to him. He was rejected by his people, hated, ridiculed, and persecuted. Jerusalem and the kingdom of Judah were destroyed although he had given them many warnings. F. B. Huey, Jr. wrote: "By God's standards he was successful, because God required only that Jeremiah obey Him by proclaiming His messages. An obedient servant of the Lord is not held accountable for the lack of response from those who hear him." [8]

There was something about Jeremiah that was like Jesus, because some people thought that Jesus was Jeremiah returned from the dead in Matthew 16:13-16. Priests spoke against Jeremiah and persecuted him; and priests spoke against Jesus and killed him. Jeremiah left a good example for teachers and preachers to follow.

God Called Jeremiah to be His Prophet
Jeremiah 1:1-19

Jeremiah was *the son of Hilkiah of the priests that were in Anathoth in the land of Benjamin*. **1:1** This community was located about three miles northeast of Jerusalem. The high priest who found the Book of the Law during Josiah's

---

[8] F. B. Huey, Jr., *Jeremiah: Bible Study Commentary*, Zondervan, p. 8

restoration of the temple in Jerusalem was named Hilkiah. (2 Kings 22:4-8)

Jeremiah began preaching *in the days of Josiah* and continued *unto the end of the eleventh year of Zedekiah*, the last king of Judah, and *unto the carrying away of Jerusalem captive.* 1:2-3

Jehoiakim and Jehoiachin were also wicked kings of Judah during this time. The prophets Zephaniah, Habakkuk, Daniel and Ezekiel also lived during this time. Daniel 9:2 mentions the prophecy of Jeremiah 29:10-14. Jeremiah prophesied in Judah for forty years, 626 - 586 BC.

When the LORD called Jeremiah to be his prophet, he said, *"Before I formed you in the womb, I knew you; and before you came forth out of the womb, I sanctified you, and I ordained you a prophet to the nations."* 1:5 Because of his foreknowledge, God was able to know what kind of man Jeremiah would be, and he ordained (appointed) him to be his prophet even before he was born. Wayne Jackson correctly states, "The text suggests the sacredness of pre-born life. Can one destroy what God is in the process of making?" [9]

Jeremiah objected. He thought he was too young. He said, *"Behold, I do not know how to speak, because I am a youth."* 1:6 [NASB] He had been preparing to serve as a priest or as a Levite, whose duties began at age 25, according to Numbers 8:24. Even if he were 20 years old at that time, he would still think of himself as a youth without the experience needed to be God's prophet. The LORD gave Jeremiah three great assurances. *First,* God had sanctified Jeremiah—he had "set him apart" to be his prophet. (1:5) *Second,* God promised, "I am with you." (1:8) *Third,* God said, "I have put my words in your mouth." (1:9)

---

[9] Wayne Jackson, *Jeremiah & Lamentations*, p. 7

God also has called us through the gospel of Christ. [10] As Christians we have been sanctified—set apart for God's service. (1 Corinthians 6:11) We are created "unto good works, which God has before ordained that we should walk in them." (Ephesians 2:10) Jesus has promised to be with us. (Matthew 28:18-20) And we have the powerful word of God to proclaim. (Hebrews 4:12)

The LORD gave Jeremiah a message of destruction and of hope not only for the nation of Judah but also for other nations. ***"See, I have this day set you over the nations and over the kingdoms, to root out, and to pull down, and to destroy, and to throw down, to build and to plant. 1:10***

Warren Wiersbe writes, "So dangerous was this message that people hearing it called Jeremiah a traitor. He would be misunderstood, persecuted, arrested, and imprisoned; and more than once, his life was in danger. The nation didn't want to hear the truth, but Jeremiah told them plainly that they were defying the Lord, disobeying the Law, and destined for judgment." [11]

God gave Jeremiah the vision of a **blooming almond branch. 1:11-12** The almond tree is the first to awake in the spring time; it is the first tree to bloom in Palestine. God was promising Jeremiah that He would be awake and would be watching over him and his work. [12]

God showed Jeremiah a vision of **a boiling pot. 1:13-16** The pot was tipped, facing away from the north and was ready to pour out its contents toward the south. The LORD said to Jeremiah, ***"Out of the north, calamity shall break forth on all the inhabitants of the land ... at the entrance of the gates of Jerusalem, against all its walls all around, and against all the cities of Judah."*** [NKJV] The army of Babylon would invade

---

[10] 2 Thessalonians 2:14

[11] Warren W. Wiersbe, *Be Decisive,* p, 20

[12] Wayne Jackson, *Jeremiah & Lamentation,* p. 8

Judah from the north. This destruction would come because they had forsaken the LORD, and had ***burned incense to other gods.***

God said, ***"Speak to them all that I command you. Do not be dismayed. ... For behold, I have made you this day a fortified city and an iron pillar. ... They will fight against you, but they shall not prevail against you. For I am with you,"*** *says the LORD,* ***"to deliver you."*** **1:17-19** ^{NKJV}

An Outline of the Book of Jeremiah

I.   God Called Jeremiah to be His Prophet, Chapter 1

II.   Three Sermons during Josiah's Reign, Chapters 2 – 6

III.   Messages during Jehoiakim's Reign, Chapters 7 – 10

IV.   Jeremiah's Inner Struggles, Chapters 11 – 20

V.   The Last King of Judah—Zedekiah, Chapters 21 -25

VI.   Blessings after Bondage, Chapters 26 – 31

VII.   Hope During Calamity, Chapters 32 – 36

VIII.   The Fall of Jerusalem, Chapters 37 – 44

IX.   The LORD Judges the Nations, Chapters 45 – 52

Review Questions on Lesson 1
Jeremiah 1

1. The theme of Jeremiah is _____.

2. How many times does Jeremiah attribute what he is saying to the LORD? _____

3. Jeremiah began his prophetic work in _____ BC, during the thirteenth year of _____ king of Judah.

4. God had determined to destroy Jerusalem and take the people of Judah as captives to Babylon because of their _____.

5. Who was the last good king of Judah? _____

6. The religious reformation in Judah did not lead the people to true _____.

7. The people returned to _____ after Josiah's death.

8. Jeremiah could be described as "The Prophet of _____, _____, and _____."

9. Why was Jeremiah successful by God's standards?
   _____

10. Jeremiah's home of Anathoth was a _____ community that was three miles northeast of the city of _____.

11. Jeremiah's prophesies were in the reigns of what four kings of Judah?

    _____

12. Name four other prophets of God that lived during the time of Jeremiah.

    _____

13. God forbad Jeremiah to _____.

14. What was Jeremiah's objection when God called him to be his prophet?

    _____

15. What three assurances did God give Jeremiah?
    (1) _____
    (2) _____
    (3) _____

16. The vision of the _____ _____ showed that God would be awake and watching over him and his work.

17. The vision of the _____ _____ showed that the destruction of Jerusalem would be coming from Babylon in the north.

18. God promised to protect Jeremiah as a _____ city. 1:18

Lesson 2

God Charges Israel with Unfaithfulness

Jeremiah 2:1 – 3:5

Three sermons by Jeremiah during the days of Josiah's reign are recorded in chapters two through six. Each one begins with God speaking to Jeremiah and instructing him what to say to the nation of Judah.

Thus says the LORD, "I remember the devotion of your youth, your love as a bride, how you followed me in the wilderness. Israel was holy to the LORD." 2:2-3 ^{ESV} The nation of Israel made a covenant with the LORD at Mount Sinai. They exchanged spiritual wedding vows. The LORD said to them, "You have seen what I did to the Egyptians, and how I bore you on eagles' wings, and brought you to myself. Now therefore, if you will obey my voice indeed, and keep my covenant, then you shall be a special treasure to me … a holy nation." (Exodus 19:4-6) And the people of Israel promised, "All that the LORD has spoken we will do." (Exodus 19:8) God led them in the wilderness for forty years. He fed them with "bread from heaven." (Exodus 16:4)

After the conquest of Canaan, Joshua led the children of Israel in the renewal of their covenant vows. (Joshua 24:1, 14-25) "And Israel served the LORD all the days of Joshua, and all the days of the elders that outlived Joshua." (Joshua 24:31) However, "there arose another generation after them, which knew not the LORD ... and the children of Israel did evil in the sight of the LORD and served the Baals." (Judges 2:10, 11) They became guilty of spiritual adultery.

Thus says the LORD, "What iniquity did your fathers find in me, that they are gone far from me?" 2:5 Because he had blessed them, they should have been seeking him, saying, "Where is the LORD?" But they did not ask, *"Where is the*

LORD who brought us up out of Egypt, who led us through the wilderness?" **2:6.** Instead, they were chasing after idols, false gods. *"The priests did not say, 'Where is the LORD?' and those who handle the law did not know Me ... the prophets prophesied by Baal and walked after things that do not profit."* **2:8** ᴺᴷᴶⱽ

"Therefore I will yet bring charges against you," says the LORD. **2:9** ᴺᴷᴶⱽ No other nation had changed its gods, even though they were "no gods", but God's people had changed their Source of Life for idols that can do nothing. The heavens would "be astonished" by the foolishness of God's people. **2:10-12**

"For my people have committed two evils: they have forsaken me, the fountain of living waters, and hewed them out cisterns, broken cisterns, that can hold no water." **2:13** They had traded the Fountain of Life for broken cisterns without water.

Is Israel a servant, a slave by birth? Why then has he become plunder? Lions have roared at him; they have growled at him. They have laid waste his land; his towns are burned and deserted. **2:14-15** ᴺᴵⱽ During the days of Ahaz king of Judah, the Edomites invaded Judah and took away captives; also, the Philistines conquered their cities. "For the LORD brought Judah low because of Ahaz." (2 Chron. 28:16-19) This humiliation was in the past, but now cities of Egypt would break the crown of Judah by subjugating the nation of Judah. The Egyptians killed Josiah the king of Judah.[13] The LORD asks, *"Have you not brought this on yourselves, by forsaking the LORD your God?"* **2:17** ᴺᴵⱽ "The greatest judgment God can send to disobedient people is to let them have their own way, and reap the sad, painful consequences of their own sins." [14] Those who do not desire to have God in

---

[13] Jeremiah 2:16, cf. 2 Kings 23:29-37
[14] Warren W. Wiersbe, *Be Decisive,* p. 26

their lives will get their own way—they will be separated "from the presence of the LORD and from the glory of his power" forever. (2 Thess. 1:7-9)

The LORD says, *"For of old time, I have broken your yoke, and burst your bands; and you said, 'I will not transgress.'"* **2:20** The reason Israel is enslaved is not God's fault. The LORD had delivered them from their bondage in Egypt and had broken the yoke of oppressing nations time and time again. Whenever Israel turned to idols, God allowed them to be enslaved. Then they would seek the LORD for help, promising "I will not transgress." But after God delivered them, they returned to *playing the harlot*. **2:20**

The LORD says, *"Yet I had planted you a noble vine, wholly a right seed: how then are you turned into the degenerate plant of a strange vine to me?"* **2:21** His people had become filthy, and no soap could make them clean. **2:22** But they were denying that they had done anything wrong, saying, *"I am not polluted!"* **2:23**

Israel was behaving like a wild female donkey in heat, according to **2:24**. *But you said, "It's no use! I love foreign gods, and I must go after them."* **2:25** ᴺᴵⱽ They had become addicted to their idolatry. Sin is addictive!

"As a thief is ashamed when he is found out, so is the house of Israel ashamed." **2:26** They had worshiped idols as their source of life, but in the time of trouble they would turn to God and say, *"Arise, and save us!"* **2:27**

And the LORD answers, *"But where are your gods that you have made for yourselves? Let them arise, if they can save you in the time of your trouble."* **2:28** ᴺᴷᴶⱽ Will material wealth, human power, and worldly wisdom save us?

"Can a virgin forget her ornaments or a bride her attire? Yet My people have forgotten Me days without number." **2:32** ᴺᴷᴶⱽ A young maiden will not forget to wear her jewelry,

and a bride will always treasure her wedding dress, but God's people had forgotten Him, their spiritual husband.

"Yet you said, 'I am innocent; surely His anger is turned away from me.' Behold, I will enter into judgment with you because you say, 'I have not sinned.'" **2:35** NASB Although Israel behaved like a prostitute, she denied her sins. First, Israel promised, "I will not transgress" (v. 20), but she did. Then she became so hardened in her sins that she declared, "I am innocent; I have not sinned."

Also, you shall be put to shame by Egypt as you were put to shame by Assyria. From this place also you shall go with your hands on your head. **2:36-37** NASB The Jews would be ashamed for trusting Egypt to deliver them from the Babylonian army. When Ahaz was king of Judah, he trusted Assyria to save Judah from Syria and the kingdom of Israel. (2 Kings 16:5-9; 17:5-6) After the Assyrians had conquered Syria and Israel, they took all the fortified cities of Judah and besieged Jerusalem. (2 Kings 18:13,17) The Jews would go to Babylon as prisoners of war.

"If a man divorces his wife and she leaves him and marries another man, should he return to her again? Would not the land be completely defiled? (Deut. 24:1-4) *But you have lived as a prostitute with many lovers*—would you now return to me? ... *Have you not just called to me: 'My Father, my friend from my youth, will you always be angry? Will your wrath continue forever?' This is how you talk, but you do all the evil you can."* **3:1-5** NIV

Jeremiah concludes his first sermon with a call for repentance. The people prayed to the LORD for deliverance from sufferings, but did not repent from their hearts. Wiersbe gives the following explanation of 3:1-5. "God had every right to reject His people, because they had abandoned Him. However, the Lord patiently called for them to return and be restored as His wife. What grace!" [15] God did not give the Jews a "certificate of divorce" when he "put away" the nation of Judah during its exile in Babylon. (Isaiah 50:1)

Review Questions on Lesson 2
Jeremiah 2:1 – 3:1

1. God remembered Israel's _____ in the wilderness when she loved him as a _____ and was _____ to the LORD. 2:1-3

2. Israel was guilty of spiritual _____.

3. Had the LORD mistreated Israel with any injustice? ____

4. Their priests that handled the law did not know _____, and their prophets prophesied by _____. 2:8

5. "They have forsaken me the fountain of _____ waters, and hewed them out cisterns, _____ cisterns that can hold _____ water." 2:13

6. God had planted Israel a _____vine, but they had become a _____ vine to him. 2:21

7. However, Israel said, "I am not _____." 2:23

8. How does Israel explain her addiction to idols in 2:25b?

   _____

9. Israel was ashamed as a _____when he is found. 2:26

---

[15] Warren W. Wiersbe, *Be Decisive,* pp. 29, 30

10. "Can a maid forget her _____ or a
    bride her _____? Yet my people have forgotten
    _____ days without number." 2:32

11. Israel became so hardened in her sins that she declared,
    "I am _____." 2:35

12. God warned Israel, "You also shall be _____
    of Egypt as you were _____ of Assyria." 2:36

13. Jeremiah warned his people that they would go from
    their homeland with their _____ on their _____.
                                                      2:37

14. Although Israel had "played the harlot," the LORD
    would restore her as his wife if she would _____
    again to him. 3:1

Lesson 3

God Calls for Repentance

Jeremiah 3:6 – 6:30

This is Jeremiah's second recorded sermon. The LORD is calling his people to return to him and be his faithful wife.

The LORD said also to me in the days of Josiah the king, "Have you seen what backsliding Israel has done? She has ... played the harlot. And I said, after she had done all these things, 'Return to Me.' But she did not return. ... Then I saw for all the causes for which backsliding Israel had committed adultery, I had put her away and given her a certificate of divorce; yet her treacherous sister Judah feared not, but went and played the harlot also." 3:6-8 NKJV After seeing what God did to Israel, Judah should have learned the importance of being faithful to the LORD, but she did not. After the fall of the northern kingdom of Israel, Manasseh king of Judah seduced the inhabitants of Jerusalem to do more evil than the nations whom the LORD had destroyed during Israel's conquest of Canaan. (2 Chronicles 33:9)

"In spite of all this her unfaithful sister Judah did not return to me with all her heart, but only in pretense," declares the LORD. 3:10 NIV Judah was unfaithful; she had broken her covenant with God. During Josiah's restoration of the worship of the LORD in the temple, their worship was not from the heart, but it was in pretense. In their hearts, they still loved their idols.

Therefore, the LORD said to Jeremiah, *"The backsliding Israel has justified herself more than treacherous Judah." 3:11* Judah had seen the consequences of unfaithfulness, and therefore Judah was more responsible. Judah should have known better than to continue in idolatry. Christians also are warned, "Keep yourselves from idols." (1 John 5:21) And there are many forms of idolatry. (Colossians 3:5)

"Go and proclaim these words toward the north, and say, 'Return, thou backsliding Israel . . . for I am merciful, says the LORD,'" **3:12** Jeremiah was to proclaim a message of hope to "the north" where the tribes of Israel had been scattered among the nations (the Gentiles) by the Assyrians. There would still be an opportunity for them to repent and return to the LORD in a spiritual marriage.

"Turn, O backsliding children," says the LORD, "for I am married to you; and I will take you one of a city, and two of a family, and I will bring you to Zion." **3:14** After the seventy years of exile in Babylon, Cyrus king of Persia made the decree that anyone among all of the LORD's people could return to Jerusalem to rebuild the city and the temple. (Ezra 1:1-4) Not all of the exiles returned—only a faithful remnant.

God's promise in Jeremiah 3:14 is completely fulfilled in Jesus Christ and his bride, the church. (Ephesians 1:6-23; 3:1-12; 5:25-27) The church is also called "mount Zion" in Hebrews 12:22-24. God says, *"I will give you shepherds ... who will feed you with knowledge and understanding."* **3:15** NKJV The shepherds would be the inspired apostles and prophets of the new covenant. (Eph. 3:1-6) *"In those days," says the LORD, "they shall say no more, 'The ark of the covenant of the LORD,' neither shall it come to mind."* **3:16** "In those days" refers to the Christian age. At that time, the old covenant of Moses would not be remembered, because it would be replaced by the new covenant of Christ. *"At that time they shall call Jerusalem the throne of the LORD; and all nations shall be gathered unto it."* **3:17** The throne of the LORD is in the New Jerusalem in heaven, and the saved of all nations will be there. (Rev. 21:1-24) Earthly Jerusalem is now in bondage, but the heavenly Jerusalem is free. (Galatians 4:25-26)

"In those days, the house of Judah shall walk with the house of Israel, and they shall come together." **3:18** God purposed "that in the dispensation of the fullness of times he might gather together in one all things in Christ." (Eph. 1:9-10) "You are all one in Christ Jesus." (Galatians 3:28)

"Return, you backsliding children, and I will heal your backsliding." **3:22** Jeremiah gives the confession that Israel must make in response to the LORD's invitation: *"Behold, we come to you; for you are the LORD our God."* **3:22b** Israel must confess that salvation does not come from their idols but from the LORD. They are to confess their shame and disgrace, saying, *"We have sinned against the LORD our God, we and our fathers, from our youth even unto this day, and have not obeyed the voice of the LORD our God."* **3:23-25**

"If you will return, O Israel," says the LORD, *"return to me; and if you will put away your abominations out of my sight, then you shall not be moved."* ... *"Break up your fallow ground."* **4:1-3** Repentance must come from deep within one's heart in order to receive God's word. The preparation of the heart should to be like that of a farmer who breaks up the unplowed ground by plowing deep in the soil before planting the seed. Using another metaphor, the LORD says, *"Circumcise yourselves to the LORD and take away the foreskins of your heart, you men of Judah ... lest my fury come forth like fire."* **4:4** "For he is not a Jew, which is one outwardly. But he is a Jew, which is one inwardly; and circumcision is that of the heart." (Romans 2:28-29) If Judah would not repent, the nation would go into Babylonian exile.

God Warns of Impending Judgment
Jeremiah 4:5 – 6:30

Jeremiah began his third sermon with a warning, saying, *"Blow the trumpet in the land!"* ... *The lion is come up from his thicket ... he is gone forth from his place to make your land desolate and your cities shall be laid waste without an inhabitant."* **4:5-7** NKJV Amos had asked rhetorically, "Shall a trumpet be blown in the city, and the people not be afraid?" (Amos 3:6) The lion symbolizes the kingdom of Babylon, which would destroy the cities of Judah and all the surrounding nations. (Daniel 7:1-4)

For this, gird you with sackcloth, lament and howl; for the fierce anger of the LORD is not turned back. **4:8** The wearing of sackcloth was a sign of repentance and great sorrow. (Matthew 11:21) Instead of heeding these warnings, the people were listening to the messages of the false prophets, who were saying, "You shall have peace." **4:10** However, the invading army would be like a devastating storm. **4:11-13.** *O Jerusalem, wash your heart from wickedness, that you may be saved.* **4:14**

"A besieging army is coming from a distant land, raising a war cry against the cities of Judah ... because she has rebelled against me," declares the LORD. "Your own conduct and actions have brought this upon you. This is your punishment. How bitter it is!" **4:16-18** NIV

Jeremiah was bold to speak the word of God, but he spoke with tears coming from a broken heart. He said, *"Oh, my anguish, my anguish! I writhe in pain. Oh, the agony of my heart!"* **4:19** NIV

God says, *"My people are foolish ... They are wise to do evil, but to do good they have no knowledge."* **4:22** NKJV

For thus has the LORD said, "The whole land shall be desolate; yet I will not make a full end." **4:27** The prophet Isaiah had predicted, "A remnant of them shall return; the destruction decreed shall overflow with righteousness." (Isaiah 10:22; Romans 9:27)

"Go up and down the streets of Jerusalem, look around and consider, search through her squares. If you can find

but one person who deals honestly and seeks the truth, I will forgive this city." 5:1 ^{NIV}

God's judgment upon Judah was justified. Not one honest man could be found in the streets of Jerusalem; no one was practicing justice and seeking the truth. They refused to receive correction. **5:3** Even "the great men" had broken the yoke and burst the bonds of their covenant with the LORD. **5:5** They had forsaken the LORD and had sworn by idols. They were like lusty stallions; every one neighed after his neighbor's wife. **5:8** They had lied about the LORD. **5:12** The people were listening to false prophets. **5:13** They had a defiant and rebellious heart. **5:23** They had mistreated the fatherless and the needy. **5:28** The priest ruled by their own power, not by God's power. **5:31** And the people supported the false prophets and the ungodly priests because that was what they wanted. **5:31**

"I will bring a nation against you from afar, O house of Israel," says the LORD. "It is a mighty nation." 5:15 "Nevertheless in those days," says the LORD, "I will not make a complete end of you." 5:18 ^{NKJV}

Behold, the word of the LORD is to them a reproach; they have no delight in it. 6:10 Instead of hearing God's warning, the people were listening to the false prophets who were saying, *"Peace, peace; when there is no peace." 6:1-14* Their hearts were hardened. Jeremiah asks, *"Were they ashamed when they had committed abominations? No, they were not at all shamed, neither could they blush." 6:15*

God pictures his people standing at the crossroads where roads went in different directions. They were thinking about which way to go. *Thus says the LORD, "Stand in the ways and see, and ask for the old paths, where the good way is, and walk in it; then you will find rest for your souls." But they said, "We will not walk in it." 6:16* ^{NKJV}

The people rejected his invitation; they would not listen to his warnings. Therefore, he would bring calamity upon them. **6:19** Their offerings and their sacrifices would be rejected, for the LORD had rejected his people. **6:20-30**

Review Questions on Lesson 3
Jeremiah 3:6 – 6:16

1. In Jeremiah's second sermon, God calls Israel to

   _____.

2. God called upon Israel to _____ to him. 3:7, 12

3. God gave backsliding Israel a certificate of _____.
                                                        3:8

4. Her sister Judah went and played the _____ also.

5. During Josiah's restoration, Judah did not return to God
   with her whole _____, but in _____.
                                                        3:10

6. "Return, thou backsliding Israel...for I am _____,"
   says, the LORD. 3:12

7. "And I will give you shepherds ...who will feed you with
   _____ and _____." 3:15

8. "In those days" refers to the _____ age. 3:16

9. God warns of impending _____ in
   Jeremiah's third sermon, 4:5 – 6:30.

10. "Blow the _____" to alert and warn the people.
                                                        4:5

11. "Your own _____ and_____ have
    brought this upon you." 4:18 NIV

12. "My people are foolish... They are wise to do _____,
    but to do _____ they have no knowledge." 4:22

13. False prophets were saying, "_____, _____."

                                                            6:15

14. God urged his people to ask for the _____ paths, where the _____ way is, and walk in it. 6:16

15. But they said, "We will _____ walk in it." 6:16

Lesson 4

Messages in Jehoiakim's Reign

Jeremiah 7 – 10

The temple sermon in chapter seven appears to be the same one that is in chapter 26. This sermon was preached in the beginning of the reign of Jehoiakim, about 608 BC.[16] His father, Josiah, was killed in battle by the Egyptians in 609 BC, and Judah became a vassal state of Egypt. Pharaoh Necho placed Jehoiakim on the throne after his brother Jehoahaz had reigned for only three months.[17] Chapter 7 emphasizes the message that was preached, and chapter 26 gives the reaction of those who heard it.

The Temple Sermon
Jeremiah 7:1 – 8:3

The LORD instructed Jeremiah to *"Stand in the gate of the LORD's house and proclaim there this word." 7:2* As the people entered the temple, perhaps during one of the great feasts, Jeremiah said, *"Hear the word of the LORD, all you of Judah that enter in at these gates to worship the LORD. Thus says the LORD, "Amend your ways and your doings, and I will cause you to dwell in this place." 7:3*

God had protected Jerusalem and the temple when it was besieged by the Assyrians many years earlier. The city was saved because Hezekiah the king trusted in the LORD and humbly prayed to him.[18] The people thought the city had been spared simply because of the temple that was within its walls. They thought of the temple as a good luck charm. God would

---

[16] Jeremiah 26:1
[17] 2 Kings 23:28-34
[18] 2 Kings 18:17 – 19:37

not allow his temple to be destroyed. This was the message being preached by the false prophets.

So the LORD said, *"Trust not in lying words, saying 'The temple of the LORD, the temple of the LORD, the temple of the LORD.'"* **7:4** Only by true repentance of their sins would God permit them to dwell in the land that he had given to their fathers. **7:5-7** *"Behold, you trust in lying words that cannot profit."* **7:8**

The LORD asks, *"Will you steal, murder, and commit adultery, and swear falsely, and burn incense to Baal, and walk after other gods ... And come and stand before me in this house, which is called by my name, and say, 'We are delivered to do all these abominations?'"* **7:9-10** Jehoiakim "did that which is evil in the sight of the LORD. according to all that his fathers had done." (2 Kings 23:37) What had his grandfather Manasseh done? He built altars to other gods in the house of the LORD, and he even set a carved image of Asherah in the temple of the LORD. (2 Kings 21:4-7) They had defiled the LORD's temple! God had not delivered them from their enemies to sin against him!

God asks, *"Has this house, which is called by my name, become a den of robbers in your eyes?"* **7:11** ᴱˢⱽ The people were using the temple as a protection for their wickedness. They were making the temple unholy! Jesus made reference to this verse after cleansing the temple in Matthew 21:13.

The LORD reminds them what he did to **Shiloh** because of their wickedness. **7:12** After the conquest of Canaan, the tabernacle was set up at Shiloh (Joshua 18:1), and it remained there for several hundred years. When the elders of Israel thought that carrying the Ark of the Covenant into battle would save them from their enemies, they were defeated and the ark was captured. (1 Samuel 4:3-11) The glory of the LORD had departed from the tabernacle and from Shiloh. (1 Samuel 4:19-22) Although the ark was returned to Israel, it was never returned to the tabernacle. The ark could not save then; the temple would not save now! Only God can save his people if they repent. (2 Peter 3:9)

He had called to them, but they refused to hear him. Therefore, the LORD would do to the temple as he had done to Shiloh. **7:13-14** God told Jeremiah not to pray for those who would not hear and obey him. **7:16** Parents led their children in worshiping other gods. The "Queen of Heaven" was a description of Ishtar, the Babylonian goddess of fertility, whose worship involved abominable obscenities.[19] The LORD's anger and fury would be poured out on Jerusalem and the temple because of these sins. **7:17-20**

The LORD is not pleased with just a sacrifice. Their sacrifices were worthless, because they were not being offered with a pure and obedient heart. They might as well eat all of the meat themselves, because God did not want any part of it. **7:21-22** The LORD said, *"Obey my voice and I will be your God, and you shall be my people. And walk in all the ways that I have commanded you that it may be well unto you."* **7:23**

Yet they did not obey or incline their ear, but followed the counsels and the dictates of their evil hearts. **7:24** ^{NKJV} They set their idols in the temple of the LORD to pollute it. **7:30** They even sacrificed their children to Molech in the Valley of Hinnom.[20] **7:31** *"Topheth* is an Aramaic word meaning 'fireplace.' The Greek word *gehenna,* meaning 'hell,' comes from the Hebrew *ge'hinnom,* the valley of Hinnom." [21] Therefore, the time would come when this place would be called *the Valley of Slaughter*, because of the great number who would die during the destruction of Jerusalem. **7:32** *And death shall be chosen rather than life* by those who would

---

[19] Warren W. Wiersbe, *Be Decisive*, p. 44
[20] 2 Kings 23:10
[21] Warren W. Wiersbe, *De Decisive,* p. 45

survive. **8:3** The siege of Jerusalem would last for one year and a half. The people in the city suffered from starvation because of the famine and from sicknesses due to the unsanitary living conditions that included dead bodies that were decomposing in the streets.

The people's reaction to Jeremiah's temple sermon is recorded in Jeremiah 26. ***When Jeremiah had made an end of speaking ... the priests and the prophets and all the people took him, saying, "You shall surely die."*** **26:8** The priests and the prophets thought Jeremiah was guilty of blasphemy for saying that Jerusalem would be destroyed like Shiloh. They wanted to kill him. **26:8** When the officials of Judah came from the royal palace to the temple to investigate the disturbance, they gave Jeremiah the opportunity to defend himself against these charges. **26:10-15**

Jeremiah said, ***"The LORD sent me to prophesy against this house and against this city all the words that you have heard."*** **26:12** He told them that if they would amend their ways and obey the LORD, God would not bring this disaster upon them. If they killed him, they would be shedding innocent blood, making their doom certain. **26:13-15**

Then the officials and all the people said to the priests and the prophets, "This man should not be sentenced to death! He has spoken to us in the name of the LORD our God." **26:16** ᴺᴵⱽ Some of the elders recalled that Micah had predicted the destruction of Jerusalem and the temple during the days of king Hezekiah; but instead of killing the prophet, the people repented and the city was spared. **26:17-19** (Micah 3:12) Unlike Urijah, who had prophesied against Jerusalem and then escaped to Egypt, Jeremiah had shown his loyalty by staying in Jerusalem to proclaim his message of doom even if it cost him his life. **26:20-23** Jeremiah also had the protection of Ahikam, the son of Shaphan the scribe. **26:24** (2 Kings 22:8-14)

Other Messages
Jeremiah 8:4 – 10:25

"They cling to deceit; they refuse to return … No one repents of his wickedness." **8:4-6** ^{NIV}

The people refused to repent because they were believing the deceitful words of false teachers. *"They have rejected the word of the LORD."* **8:9** *"Were they ashamed when they had committed abomination? No! They were not at all ashamed; neither could they blush."* **8:12** The LORD asks, *"Why have they provoked me to anger with their carved images and with their foreign idols?"* **8:29** ^{ESV}

When people today reject God's word, is not the LORD provoked to anger? He sends global warming, storms, plagues and wars. He is sounding trumpets of warning and pouring out bowls of wrath. (Revelation 8-11; 15-16) God has predicted, **"And they did not repent of their murders nor their sorceries nor of their immorality nor their thefts." Revelation 9:21** ^{NKJV}

Jeremiah describes a sad condition, *"The harvest is past, the summer is ended, and we are not saved!"* **8:20** He asks, *"Is there no balm in Gilead?"* **8:22** They had failed to seek healing from the LORD, the Great Physician.

Jeremiah says, *"Oh that my head were waters, and my eyes a fountain of tears, that I might weep day and night for the slain of the daughter of my people! Oh that I had in the wilderness a lodging place…that I might leave my people, and go from them."* **9:1-2** He longs to get away from their sinful environment, but he must stay and proclaim God's word.

Jeremiah asks, *"Why does the land perish and burn up like a wilderness?"* The LORD answers, *"Because they have forsaken My law … they have walked according to the dictates of their own hearts."* **9:12-14** ^{NKJV} Therefore, God would *feed them, even this people, with wormwood and give them water of gall to drink.* **9:15** They would be scattered among the nations and consumed by the sword. **9:16** They would be plundered and cast out of their houses. **9:19** Their children and young men would be killed. **9:21**

Thus says the LORD, "Let not a wise man boast of his wisdom, let not the mighty man boast of his might, let not the rich man boast of his riches; but let him who boasts boast of this, that he understands and knows Me, that I am the LORD who exercises lovingkindness, justice and righteousness on the earth." **9:23-24** ^{NASB} (See 1 Cor. 1:31.)

"Behold, the days come," declares the LORD, "that I will punish all who are circumcised and yet uncircumcised ... all the house of Israel are uncircumcised in the heart. **9:25-26** (See Romans 2:29.)

In the tenth chapter, Jeremiah shows the foolishness of serving idols and the wisdom of worshiping the LORD God. An idol, the work of man's hands, cannot speak; it must be carried about and supported because it has no power. *"Be not afraid of them, for they cannot do evil, neither also is it in them to do good."* **10:1-5**

"But the LORD is the true God; he is the living God, and an everlasting king. At his wrath, the earth shall tremble; and the nations shall not be able to abide his indignation. ... He has made the earth by his power, he has established the world by his wisdom, and has stretched out the heavens at his discretion." **10:10, 12**

Jeremiah concludes with this confession and prayer:
"O LORD, I know that the way of man is not in himself;
it is not in man that walks to direct his steps.
O LORD, correct me."
-- Jeremiah 10:23-24a

Review Questions on Lesson 4
Jeremiah 7 - 10

1. Why did the people think that Jerusalem was protected from invading armies? 7:1-4 _____

2. Only by true _____ would God permit them to dwell in Jerusalem. 7:5-7

3. "Behold, you trust in _____ words that cannot profit." 7:8

4. God's house had become "a _____ of _____" according to Jeremiah 7:11.

5. In the time of the Judges, the _____ of the Lord had departed from the tabernacle in Shiloh when the _____ of the covenant was captured by the Philistines. 7:12 and 1 Samuel 4:17-22

6. The LORD would do to the _____ as he had done to Shiloh. 7:13-14

7. Why did God tell Jeremiah not to pray for "this people"? 7:16 _____

8. Who was "The Queen of Heaven" that the Jews were worshiping? 7:18 _____

_____

9. Why were their sacrifices worthless? 7:21-22

_____

10. What did God promise if they would obey him? 7:23

_____

_____

11. How had they polluted the temple? 7:30

_____

12. They sacrificed their children to _____ in the Valley of Hinnom. 7:31

13. The _____ and the _____ led the people in seeking Jeremiah's death. 26:8

14. Why did the officials (the princes) say that Jeremiah should not be put to death? _____

_____

15. No one repented of his _____. 8:6 Nor did they know how to _____. 8:12

16. "The harvest is _____, the summer is _____ and we are not _____." 8:20

17. "Is there no _____ in Gilead?" 8:22

18. "Oh, that my head were _____, and my eyes a fountain of _____, that I might _____ day and night for the slain daughter of my people. 9:1

19. "They have walked according to the _____ of their own hearts." 9:14 ᴺᴷᴶⱽ

20. They would perish because "they have walked according to the _____ of their own hearts." 9:14 ᴺᴷᴶⱽ

21. "Let not the wise man glory in his _____." 9:23

22. "O LORD, I know the way of man is not in _____;
    it is not in man that walks to _____ his steps.
    O LORD, _____ me." 10:23-24

NOTES

Lesson 5

They Had Broken God's Covenant

Jeremiah 11 – 15

When Jehoiakim became king, the people returned to idolatry, rebelling against the reforms of Josiah. Due to the hardness of their wicked hearts, God's judgment upon them was now certain. In the third year of the reign of Jehoiakim king of Judah, Nebuchadnezzar king of Babylon came to Jerusalem and besieged it. (Daniel 1:1) King Jehoiakim came under the rule of the king of Babylon. Daniel and other talented young men of Judah were the first captives to be taken to Babylon. The date was 606 BC.

Thus says the LORD *God of Israel, "Cursed is the man who does not obey the words of this covenant, which I commanded your fathers in the day I brought them out of the land of Egypt."* **11:3-4** The curses for disobeying the covenant are given in Deuteronomy 28:15 – 29:29. God had said, *"Obey My voice, and do according to all that I command you; so shall you be My people, and I will be your God."* **11:4** But they did not obey him, because *"everyone followed the dictates of his evil heart."* **11:8** NKJV

There was a **conspiracy**. **11:9** The LORD said, *"They are turned back to the iniquities of their forefathers who refused to hear my words; and they went after other gods to serve them; the house of Israel and the house of Judah have broken my covenant which I made with their fathers."* **11:10** They had broken God's covenant. Therefore, He said, *"I will surely bring calamity on them which they will not be able to escape; and though they shall cry out to Me, I will not listen to them."* **11:11** NKJV The people then will cry out to their idols, *"but they shall not save them at all in the time of their trouble."* **11:12** Judah had as many gods as it had cities. **11:13**

The LORD again instructed Jeremiah, *"Do not pray for this people nor offer any plea or petition for them, because I will not listen."* **11:14** ^{NIV}

The LORD's people were like *a green olive tree, fair, and of a goodly fruit.* **11:16** But God would cause a storm to come against it. Lightning would set it on fire, and the wind would break its branches. *"For the LORD of hosts who planted you, has pronounced evil against you, for the evil of the house of Israel and of the house of Judah, which they have done against themselves to provoke me to anger in offering incense to Baal."* **11:17** In Romans 11:17-24, an olive tree represents God's people; and branches are grafted in because of faith, and branches are broken off because of unbelief.

Jeremiah's First Lament
Jeremiah 11:18-23

There was a plot against Jeremiah, but he says, *"Because the LORD revealed their plot to me, I knew it, for at that time he showed me what they were doing. I had been like a gentle lamb led to the slaughter."* **11:18-19** ^{NIV} His own people, in the priestly community of Anathoth, were seeking to kill him. Jeremiah cries to the LORD, *"Let me see your vengeance on them; for to you I have revealed my cause."* **11:20** God's vengeance would come upon these persecutors. They would be killed, their sons and daughters would die by famine, and no remnant would be left. **11:21-23**

Jeremiah's Second Lament
Jeremiah 12:1-6

Jeremiah asks, *"Why does the way of the wicked prosper?"* **12:1** *How long will the land mourn, and the herbs of every field wither? The beasts and the birds are consumed, for the wickedness of those who dwell there.* **12:4** ^{NKJV} God answers Jeremiah in verses **5-6**. He says the worse is yet to come. Jeremiah is not to trust even his brothers in his father's house when they speak friendly words to him. Warren Wiersbe said, "Jeremiah was asking, '*How* can I get out of this?' But he should have been asking, '*What* can I get out of this?' God's servants don't live by explanations; they live by promises. Each new challenge helped Jeremiah develop his faith and grow more mature." [22]

God Will Punish the Wicked
Jeremiah 12:7-13

God says, *"I have forsaken my house; I have left my heritage. I have given the dearly beloved of my soul into the hand of her enemies."* **12:7** God had forsaken his temple and abandoned his people to be punished by their enemies. Like a lion in the forest, his heritage had roared against him. Therefore, *the sword of the LORD shall devour from the one end of the land even to the other end of the land; no flesh shall have peace.* **12:12**

A Promise of Restoration
Jeremiah 12:14-17

God promises, *"I will return, and have compassion on them, and will bring them again, every man to his heritage, and every man to his land."* **12:14-15** The Babylonians were defeated by the Medes and Persians in 539 BC. Three years later, the Jews were able to return to their homeland.

God made this promise concerning the Gentile nations, *"If they will diligently learn the ways of my people, to swear by my name, 'The LORD lives,' as they taught my people to swear by Baal, then shall they be built in the midst of my people."* **12:16** They would become part of God's spiritual temple, his church. (Eph. 2:11-22; 1 Pet. 2:5)

---

[22] Warren W. Wiersbe, *Be Decisive*, p. 62

"But if they will not obey, I will utterly pluck up and destroy that nation," says the LORD. **12:17** The only nation that will survive is God's "holy nation" that has been called "out of darkness" into God's "light." (1 Peter 2:9)

The Lesson of the Linen Waistband
Jeremiah 13:1-11

God said to Jeremiah, *"Go and buy yourself a linen waistband and put it around your waist, but do not put it in water."* **13:1** ^{NASB} His wearing the waistband symbolized the closeness God desired to have with his people. Jeremiah was not to wash the linen garment to represent the increasing wickedness of the people. He was told to go to the Euphrates River in Babylon and hide the waistband in a crevice in a rock. "After many days" the LORD instructed him to retrieve the hidden garment. It was worthless!

Thus says the LORD, "After this manner I will mar the pride of Judah, and the great pride of Jerusalem." **13:9** In their exile in Babylon, the people would be humbled and come to understand their need to be close to God and to be cleansed by him. This is the lesson of the linen waistband.

The Lesson of the Filled Wine Bottles
Jeremiah 13:12-14

Thus says the LORD God of Israel, "Every bottle shall be filled with wine." **13:12** The people knew the proverb: *"Every bottle shall be filled with wine,"* promising peace and prosperity. But God says, *"I will fill all the inhabitants of this land, even the kings that sit on David's throne, and the priests, and the prophets, and all the inhabitants of Jerusalem with drunkenness."* **13:13** They would be filled with the wrath of God like staggering drunkards. Idolaters "will drink of the wine of God's fury, which has been poured out full strength into the cup of his wrath." ^{NIV} (Rev. 14:9-10)

The Threat of Captivity
Jeremiah 13:15-27

Hear and give ear; do not be proud, for the LORD has spoken. ... But if you will not hear it, my soul shall weep in secret for your pride ... because the LORD's flock has been taken captive. Say to the king and to the queen mother, "Humble yourselves; sit down, for your rule shall collapse, the crown of your glory." **13:15-18** ^{NKJV}After Jehoiakim died, his son Jehoiachin replaced him on the throne, and he also did evil in the sight of the LORD. (2 Kings 24:6, 8-9). After reigning only three months, Jerusalem was besieged. Jehoiachin and his mother were carried into Babylonian captivity.[23] Ezekiel the prophet was among the ten thousand captives taken to Babylon at this time, 597 BC.

The Sword, The Famine & The Pestilence
Jeremiah 14

A severe drought had come upon the land of Judah. God's use of the weather was promised in Deuteronomy [24] and had been demonstrated in the time of Elijah.[25] Jeremiah pleads to the LORD on behalf of his people, *"Do not leave us!"* **14:7-9** But, it's too late! Prayers, fasts, and offerings will do no good. God would *consume them by the sword, and by the famine, and by the pestilence.* **14:12**

The false prophets were promising peace and assuring the people that these calamities would not come. The LORD responded, *"The prophets prophesy lies in my name ... they prophesy to you a false vision...the deceit of their heart."* **14:14** At that time, and even now, false teachers "bring on themselves swift destruction." (2 Peter 2:1) *"By the sword and famine shall those prophets be consumed."* **14:15**

---

[23] 2 Kings 24:8, 10-15
[24] Deuteronomy 28:24
[25] James 5:17-18

Those who believed the lies of their prophets would suffer death by the sword and by starvation, and *they will have no one to bury them.* **14:16** Jeremiah asks the LORD, *"Have you utterly rejected Judah?"* **14:19** He asks God not to despise his nation for the sake of his name and for the throne of his glory and for his covenant. **14:20-22**

God's Judgment upon Judah Will Stand
Jeremiah 15:1-9

The LORD tells Jeremiah that he is tired of showing pity to Judah. He would not change his mind even if Moses and Samuel interceded for the nation as they had done in times past. [26] God said, *"Cast them out of my sight, and let them go forth."* **15:1** Some would go into captivity. He asks, *"Who shall have pity upon you, O Jerusalem?"* **15:5-6**

Jeremiah's Third Lament
Jeremiah 15:10-21

Jeremiah laments his being rejected by his people. He regrets his birth, because his countrymen consider him a man of strife and contention. Everyone curses him without cause. **15:10** The LORD reassures him that when the Babylonians come to destroy the land, they would treat him well. **15:11**

Jeremiah resumes his complaint, *"O LORD, you know! Remember me, and visit me, and revenge me of my persecutors. Take me not away from your longsuffering. Know that for your sake I have suffered rebuke. ... Thy word was to me the joy and rejoicing of my heart."* **15:15-16** However, Jeremiah says, *"I sat alone because of your hand, for you have filled me with indignation."* **15:17** He asks, *"Why is my pain perpetual, and my wound incurable?"* **15:18** He

---

[26] Exodus 32:11-14 and 1 Samuel 7:5-9

feels that God has failed to keep his promise to protect him (1:18-19).

NIV records it: *"If you repent, I will restore you that you may serve me; if you utter worthy, not worthless words, you will be my spokesman."* **15:19**

Jeremiah needed to repent of his negative thoughts, and God would restore him as his courageous prophet. Our faith in God is like the gold that is separated by fire from the dross (our human sufferings and fears). (1 Peter 1:7) The trials of persecution can strengthen and purify our faith. (James 1:2-4; Romans 5:1-5) Jeremiah was to bring the people back to God, instead of becoming like them in their distrust of God. The LORD again promised him, *"I am with you to save you and to deliver you."* **15:20**

Review Questions on Lesson 5
Jeremiah 11 – 15

1. God's people had broken the _____ that their fathers made with God by serving other gods. 11:10

2. In the _____ year of Jehoiakim, the city of Jerusalem was besieged, and the first captives were taken to Babylon. Daniel 1:1

3. A _____ was placed upon the man who did not obey the words of the covenant. 11:3

4. In 11:4, what blessing was promised to them if they obeyed God's voice? _____

    _____

5. "Yet they did not obey or incline their ear, but everyone followed the _____ of his evil heart." 11:8 NKJV

6. Because they had broken the covenant, the LORD would "bring _____ upon them." 11:11

7. Israel is compared to a green _____ tree in Jeremiah in 11:16-17.

8. Who was seeking to kill Jeremiah? 11:21

    _____

9. What question does Jeremiah ask in 12:1?

    _____

10. The lesson of the linen waistband (sash) is that the exile in Babylon would teach them to be _____ to God and to be _____ by him. 13:1-11

11. The land of Judah was having a severe _____ because of their _____. 14:1-9

12. God would consume them by the _____, the _____ and the _____. 14:12

13. False prophets prophesy _____ in God's name. 14:14

14. Jeremiah asks God not to despise his nation for the sake of God's _____, and for the _____ of his glory, and for his _____with them. 14:21

15. In 15:1, the LORD would not change his mind about punishing his people even if what two men interceded for the nation? 15:1 _____ and _____

16. The LORD said, "I am weary of _____." 15:6

17. In 15:10-21, Jeremiah regrets his _____, because he is considered a man of _____ and _____. Everyone _____ him.

18. God answered Jeremiah's discouragement saying, "If you _____, then you shall stand before me." 15:19

NOTES

Lesson 6

The Inner Struggles of Jeremiah

Jeremiah 16 – 20

A view into the heart of Jeremiah is seen in this section of the book. This lesson contains his remaining three laments in 17:14-18, 18:18-23 and 20:7-18. These laments reveal his inner struggles during times of personal sufferings. They are sources of encouragement to faithful teachers and preachers in their efforts to proclaim God's word.

The Message of Jeremiah's Unusual Life
Jeremiah 16:1-13

The word of the LORD also came to me, saying, "You shall not take a wife, nor shall you have sons or daughters in this place. For thus says the LORD concerning the sons and daughters who are born in this place, and concerning their mothers who bore them and their fathers who begot them in this land: "They shall die gruesome deaths… They shall be consumed by the sword and by famine." 16:1-4 NKJV

God did not allow Jeremiah to marry and have a family as a symbolic act, because the sons and daughters of Jewish families would either die by the sword or starve to death in the coming Babylonian invasion. Also, Jeremiah was not to attend funerals, feasts or weddings (**16:5, 8, 9**) because God had removed his peace and comfort from the nation. God's judgment upon them would be so terrible that the people would not be able to express joy or grief.

The people would ask, *"Why has the LORD pronounced all this great disaster against us?"* Then Jeremiah would answer, *"Because your fathers have forsaken Me" says the LORD, "they have walked after other gods ... and you have done worse than your fathers ... each one follows the dictates of his own evil heart, so no one listens to Me."* **16:10-12** ^{NKJV}

The Restoration of True Israel
Jeremiah 16:14-21

The LORD promises a second exodus that will be greater than the exodus from Egypt. He will bring up *the children of Israel from the land of the north, and from all the lands where he had driven them.* He said, *"I will bring them again into their land that I gave to their fathers."* **16:14-15** But for the present time, there was no escaping the LORD's wrath. He will send out many *"fishermen"* to catch them and *"hunters"* to hunt them down, and *"repay them double for their wickedness and their sin."* **16:16-18** ^{NIV} Jeremiah confesses that the LORD is his **strength**, his **fortress**, and his **refuge** in the time of affliction. He predicts, *"The Gentiles shall come to You from the ends of the earth,"* and they will renounce their worthless idols. **16:19-20**, ^{NKJV} This prophecy is fulfilled in Christ and the gospel. (1 Thessalonians 1:5-9) The "second exodus" is completely fulfilled in all those who are brought out of the kingdom of darkness into the kingdom of Christ, "in whom we have redemption through his blood, the forgiveness of sins." (Colossians 1:12-14)

Messages about the Heart of Man
Jeremiah 17:1-13

The sin of Judah is written with a pen of iron...on the tablet of their heart. **17:1** *Thus says the LORD, "Cursed is the man who trusts in man and makes flesh his strength; whose heart departs from the LORD."* **17:5** *"Blessed is the man who trusts in the LORD and whose hope is the LORD, for he shall be like a tree planted by the waters."* **17:7-8** *"The heart is deceitful above all things, and desperately wicked; who can know it? I, the LORD, search the heart, I test the mind, even to give every man according to his ways."* **17:9-**

10 NKJV Those who depart from the living God shall have their names written in the earth which will perish, *because they have forsaken the LORD, the fountain of living waters.* **17:13**

Jeremiah's Fourth Lament
Jeremiah 17:14-18

Heal me, O LORD, and I shall be healed; save me, and I shall be saved. **17:14** The people were mocking Jeremiah, saying, *"Where is the word of the LORD? Let it come now!"* **17:15** They were making fun of him because his predictions of doom had not come to pass. Yet, Jeremiah had been a faithful shepherd by giving them God's warning. He says, *"Let them be ashamed who persecute me, but do not let me be put to shame; let them be dismayed, but do not let me be dismayed. Bring on them the day of doom."* **17:18**

The Sermon about the Sabbath
Jeremiah 17:19-27

The LORD instructed Jeremiah to preach a sermon about the Sabbath. They were to keep the Sabbath holy by not doing any work on that day. Fire would devour Jerusalem if they did not observe the Sabbath.

The Potter and the Clay
Jeremiah 18:1-17

The LORD is the potter; Judah is the clay. If the clay is marred in the potter's hand as he makes a vessel, he has the right to make the clay into a different vessel. God said, *"If that nation against whom I have spoken turns from its evil, I will relent of the disaster that I thought to bring upon it."* **18:8** NKJV God has the power to destroy a nation and to build it. However, the people rejected God's offer. **18: 10-17**

Jeremiah's Fifth Lament
Jeremiah 18:18-23

Jeremiah asks the LORD, *"Shall evil be repaid for good?"* **18:20** ᴺᴷᴶⱽ His warnings of doom were intended for their good. Jeremiah was calling his nation to repentance and salvation. But they had dug a pit for his life.

The Sign of the Broken Clay Jar
Jeremiah 19:1-15

The LORD instructed Jeremiah to get a clay jar and take some of the elders and some of the priests to **the valley of Ben-Hinnom**. **19:1** This valley was on the south side of Jerusalem. After their going there Jeremiah said, **"Thus says the LORD of hosts, the God of Israel: 'Behold, I am about to bring a calamity upon this place, at which the ears of everyone that hears of it will tingle. Because they have forsaken Me and made this an alien place and have burned sacrifices in it to other gods ... and because they have filled this place with the blood of the innocent and have built the high places of Baal to burn their sons in the fire as burnt offerings to Baal..., therefore, behold, the days are coming," declares the LORD, "when this place will no longer be called Topheth or the valley of Ben-Hinnom, but the valley of Slaughter." 19:2-6** ᴺᴬˢᴮ

The people had forsaken the LORD. They had engaged in sexual immoral acts in their worship of Baal, and then they offered their babes as burnt offerings to Baal. **Topheth** means fireplace or fire pit. The LORD said that it would be called the Valley of Slaughter. **19:6** (See the notes on Jeremiah 7:31-32.) During the siege of Jerusalem, the people would be so desperate for food that they would eat the flesh of their own dead sons and daughters. **19:9** Jeremiah was to break the clay jar in the sight of the men with him and say, *"Thus says the LORD of hosts: 'Even so I will break this people and this city,* *as one breaks a potter's vessel, that cannot be made whole again; and they shall bury them in Topheth till there is no place to bury.'"* **19:11**

Then Jeremiah returned to the temple court and said to all the people, *"Thus says the LORD of hosts, the God of Israel, 'Behold, I will bring on this city and on all her towns all the doom that I have pronounced against it."* **19:15**

Jeremiah's Sixth Lament
Jeremiah 20:1-18

When the chief temple officer heard that Jeremiah prophesied these things, he had Jeremiah beaten and put in stocks for a day. **20:1-3** Jeremiah said, *"O LORD, you have deceived me, and I was deceived; you are stronger than I and have prevailed; I am in derision daily; everyone mocks me."* **20:7** God had talked Jeremiah into being his prophet, but Jeremiah was thinking his work was useless, for it had brought him only ridicule. So, he said, *"I will not make mention of Him, nor speak anymore in His name."* Then he confessed, *"But His word was in my heart like a burning fire shut up in my bones; I was weary of holding it back, and I could not."* **20:9** ᴺᴷᴶⱽ He had to be God's spokesman.

Jeremiah's acquaintances watched for his stumbling, but he said, *"The LORD is with me as a mighty, awesome One. Therefore my persecutors will stumble, and will not prevail."* **20:11** ᴺᴷᴶⱽ Jeremiah would go from his despair to trusting in God, and then back to hurting in his afflictions and questioning, *"Why did I come forth from the womb to see labor and sorrow, that my days should be consumed with shame?"* **20:18** ᴺᴷᴶⱽ

Review Questions on Lesson 6
Jeremiah 16 – 20

1. God did not allow Jeremiah to _____ nor to attend _____ or _____.
16:1-13

2. Jeremiah predicted that the _____ would come to the LORD, and they would renounce their worthless _____. 16:19-20

3. "Cursed is the man who trusts in _____ and makes flesh his strength, whose heart departs from the LORD." 17:5 NKJV

4. "The heart is _____ above all things and desperately _____." 17:9

5 "I, the LORD, search the _____, I test the _____." 17:10

6. The LORD compares himself to a _____ and Judah to _____ in 18:1-11.

7. "If that _____ against whom I have spoken turns from its _____, I will relent of the _____ that I thought to bring upon it." 18:8 NKJV

8. Jeremiah asks, "Shall _____ be repaid for _____? For they have dug a pit for my _____." 18:20 NKJV

9. For what three reasons did the LORD bring a calamity upon the valley of Ben-Hinnom (Son of Hinnom) in 19:2-5?
    (1) _____
    (2) _____
    (3) _____

10. What was the new name that God gave to the valley of Ben-Hinnom (Son of Hinnom)? 19:6

    _____

11. What did the temple officer do to Jeremiah? 20:1-2

    _____

12. In his last lament, he says, "I am in _____ daily; everyone _____ me." 20:7

13. Then Jeremiah said, "I will not make _____ of Him, nor speak anymore in His _____. But His word was in my _____ like a _____ _____ shut up in my _____; I was weary of _____ __ _____, and I could not." 20:9 NKJV

14. "But the LORD is _____ me as a _____, awesome One. Therefore, my persecutors will _____ and not _____." 20:11 NKJV

NOTES

Lesson 7

The Last King of Judah— Zedekiah

Jeremiah 21 – 25

The last king in the lineage of David to reign in Jerusalem was Zedekiah, 597 to 586 BC. As the Babylonian army came against Jerusalem, Zedekiah asked Jeremiah *"to inquire of the LORD for us."* **21:1-2**

In chapter 22, Jeremiah went to see Zedekiah urging him to change his ways in order to avoid much suffering. He reminded Zedekiah that the word of the LORD had been proven true concerning three other kings of Judah.

In chapter 23, God promises to keep his covenant with David by raising up a Branch of righteousness, the Messiah. He would reign over the remnant of Judah and Israel. But during Zedekiah's time, their whole land would become "a desolation and an astonishment", and they would "serve the king of Babylon seventy years." (25:11)

Jerusalem's Doom Is Certain
Jeremiah 21

Zedekiah refused to pay tribute to Babylon. He rebelled in 588 BC. And Nebuchadnezzar king of Babylon came with his army against Jerusalem.   Zedekiah sent two messengers to Jeremiah hoping that the LORD would save Jerusalem as he had done in the days of Hezekiah and Isaiah. (2 Kings 18-19) Instead of promising to help Zedekiah, the LORD said, *"I myself will fight against you with an outstretched hand and with a strong arm, even in anger and in fury and in great wrath."* **21:5**   God would deliver Zedekiah into the hand of the king of Babylon. **21:7**

The LORD offered a way of salvation for the people. He said, *"Behold, I set before you the way of life and the way of death. He that abides in this city shall die by the sword, and by the famine and by the pestilence; but he that goes out and falls to the Chaldeans that besiege you, he shall live."* **21:8-9** Those who surrendered to the Chaldean rulers of Babylon would be spared. The king of Babylon would burn Jerusalem with *fire.* **21:10** The LORD appealed to the house of the king of Judah to execute justice and to deliver the oppressed. **21:11-12** He concluded, *"I will punish you according to the fruit of your doings."* **21:14**

The LORD's Last Appeal to Zedekiah
Jeremiah 22

The LORD instructed Jeremiah to make one final appeal to Zedekiah to do right. The LORD swore by himself that if the king refused to obey, *his house* would become *a desolation.* **22:1-5** God had promised to establish David's dynasty forever. (2Samuel 7) Not only was the king's palace destroyed by the Babylonians but his throne became **a desolation.** No king would sit on David's throne until the coming of Christ, who was given "the throne of his father David." (Luke 1:26-32)

Jerusalem would be destroyed, *"because they have forsaken the covenant of the LORD their God, and worshiped other gods and served them."* **22:8-9** Jeremiah reminded the king of three messages that the LORD had spoken in the past: the first concerning Shallum (**22:11-12**), the second concerning Jehoiakim (**22:13-19**) and the third was about Coniah (**22:24-30**).

Shallum was the first name of Jehoahaz. (1 Chron. 3:15) When Josiah was killed in a battle against the Egyptians, "the people of the land took Jehoahaz the son of Josiah and made him king in his father's stead." (2 Kings 23:30)

After reigning only three months, Pharaoh Necho put him in prison in Riblah in Syria while making his brother Jehoiakim king. Then Pharaoh took Jehoahaz (Shallum) to Egypt. The prophecy of the LORD by Jeremiah concerning Shallum was *"He shall not return here anymore, but he shall die in the place where they have led him captive, and shall see this land no more."* **22:11-12** NJKV And "he died there" in Egypt. (2 Kings 23:34) Most of the Jews that went into Babylon as captives would see the land of Judah no more. The LORD has spoken!

Jehoiakim reigned eleven years in Jerusalem, and "he did that which was evil in the sight of the LORD." (2 Kings 23:36-37) In the third year of his reign, Nebuchadnezzar came to Jerusalem and besieged the city and took the first captives to Babylon, including Daniel. (Daniel 1:1-7). During his reign, Judah was attacked by bands of Syrians, Moabites and other nearby countries allied with Babylon. (2 Kings 24:1-2) "During a time of international crisis, Jehoiakim was more concerned about building his own spacious palace than he was building a righteous kingdom, and he even used unpaid Jewish slave labor to do it!" [27] So, the LORD's message to Jehoiakim was *"Woe to him who builds his house by unrighteousness and his chambers by injustice, who uses his neighbor's service without wages and gives him nothing for his work."* **22:13-17** NKJV Therefore, Jehoiakim would not be lamented in his death. **22:18-19**. Neither would the people weep for Zedekiah, who also was guilty of injustices. (cf. 22:3)

There would be weeping for the fall of Jerusalem, which is called "Lebanon" because the cedars of Lebanon were used extensively in its buildings. **22:20-23** In their prosperity the LORD spoke to them, but they said, *"I will not hear."* Now they would go into captivity!

---

[27] Warren W. Wiersbe, *Be Decisive*, p. 102

The third message to Zedekiah was about Coniah. **22:24-30** "Coniah" is a shortened form of Jeconiah, another name for Jehoiachin, the son of Jehoiakim. (1 Chronicles 3:16) He was only eighteen years old when he became king. "And he did that which was evil in the sight of the LORD." He reigned for just over three months before he and his mother were deported to Babylon, and he was replaced by his uncle Zedekiah. (2 Kings 24:8-17). If Jehoiachin were the signet ring on God's right hand, the LORD would remove it. **22:24** The LORD said to him, *"I will cast you out, and your mother that bore you, into another country ... and there you shall die."* **22:26** And He did! The message concludes with a very important prophecy. *Thus says the LORD, "Write this man childless ... for no man of his seed shall prosper, sitting upon the throne of David, and ruling anymore in Judah."* **22:30** Although Jeconiah (Jehoiachin) had seven sons, [28] he was counted *as* childless when it came to having a descendant on the throne in earthly Jerusalem. Wayne Jackson says, "This passage presents a formidable problem for millennialists. For the fact is, Jesus Christ was descended from Jehoiachin, via Shealtiel (1 Chronicles 3:17), both regally (Matthew 1:1-16) and physically (Luke 3:23-38). As a descendant of Jehoiachin, therefore, the Lord will never be able to sit on David's literal throne, and prosper, reigning in Judah!" [29]

The LORD Our Righteousness
Jeremiah 23

God condemns Judah's leaders. *"Woe to the shepherds who destroy and scatter the sheep of My pasture!* Then He promises, *"But I will gather the remnant of My flock out of all the countries where I have driven them."* **23:1-3** NKJV The LORD uses the word "remnant" nineteen times in this book.

---

[28] 1 Chronicles 3:17
[29] Wayne Jackson, *Jeremiah & Lamentations,* p. 55

"Behold, the days are coming," declares the LORD, *"when I shall raise up for David a righteous Branch; and He will reign as king and act wisely and do justice and righteousness in the land. In His days Judah will be saved, and Israel will dwell securely; and this is His name by which He will be called 'The* LORD *our righteousness.'"* **23:5-6** ^{NASB} This is a messianic prophecy fulfilled in Christ. Our deliverance from sin by Christ will be greater than Israel's deliverance from Egyptian bondage. **23:7-8**

Jeremiah said, *"My heart within me is broken because of the prophets. ... For both prophet and priest are profane; yes, in my house I have found their wickedness,"* says the LORD. **23:9, 11** *"They strengthen also the hands of evildoers, that none returns from his wickedness."* **23:14** The false prophets *speak a vision of their own heart, and not out of the mouth of the* LORD. **23:16** *And to everyone who walks according to the dictates of his own heart, they say, 'No evil shall come upon you.'"* **23:17** ^{NKJV} For the eighth time in the book of Jeremiah, the LORD condemns following "the dictates" of one's own heart. He emphasizes over and over again that we must not look within ourselves for truth, but we must listen to His word. The LORD has spoken!

"Am I a God at hand," says the LORD, *"and not a God afar off? ... Do I not fill heaven and earth?"* **23:23, 24** God affirms his omnipresence with these questions. We can draw near to God "in full assurance of faith." (Heb. 10:22) He promises the faithful, "I will never leave you nor forsake you." (Heb. 13:5) The LORD hears the lies of false prophets. He says, *"I have heard what the prophets said, that prophesy lies in my name, saying, 'I have dreamed, I have dreamed!'"* **23:25** We hear false prophets today, saying, "I had a revelation." God's word is powerful; he compares it to *a fire* and *a hammer* in **23:29**. The word of the LORD should be taken seriously. "Take heed what you hear." (Mark 4:24)

The Two Baskets of Figs
Jeremiah 24

The LORD showed Jeremiah a vision of two baskets of figs. This was after Jehoiachin was taken to Babylon in 597 BC. (2 Kings 24:15) The basket of **good figs** represented those who were carried away captive of Judah *for their good.* **24:5** Those who would return to their homeland as God's people would *return to him with their whole heart.* **24:6-7** The basket of **bad figs** represented king Zedekiah, his officials, and those who remained in Judah, as well as those who fled to Egypt. **24:8** They would become objects of ridicule and cursing among the kingdoms of the earth. **24:9** They would be consumed by the sword, the famine, and the pestilence. **24:10**

Seventy Years of Desolation
Jeremiah 25

The year was 605 BC, the fourth year of Jehoiakim's reign. **25:1** Daniel and other talented young men had been taken captive to Babylon the year before. Jeremiah had been preaching for 23 years, but the people had not listened **25:3** The LORD decreed, *"This whole land shall be a desolation and an astonishment, and these nations shall serve the king of Babylon seventy years. And it will come to pass, when the seventy years are accomplished, that I will punish the king of Babylon."* **25:11-12** All the nations would drink the wine of God's wrath, including Judah, Egypt, Philistia, Edom, Moab, Ammon, Phoenicia, and Arabia. **25:15-38**

Review Questions on Lesson 7
Jeremiah 21 – 25

1. The last king in David's dynasty to reign in Jerusalem was _____. 21:1

2. Who would fight against the king of Judah "with a strong arm, even in anger and in fury and in great wrath"? 21:4-5 _____

3. Those remaining in the city of Jerusalem would be choosing the way of _____.

4. Those who surrendered to the enemy would be choosing the way of _____.

5. Shallum was the first name of_____.

6. Where did Shallum die? _____

7. What king built a spacious palace using unpaid labor?

   _____

8. What king was also guilty of similar injustices?

   _____

9. Coniah is a shortened form of Jeconiah, another name for what king of Judah? _____

10. The LORD compares his removing Coniah as king with removing a _____ _____.

11. What is significant about the prophecy concerning Coniah that "none of his descendants shall prosper, sitting on the throne of David, and ruling anymore in Judah"? _____

12. God says, "I will gather the _____ of my flock out of all the countries where I have driven them." 23:3

13. God would keep his promise to David by raising up a Branch of _____.

14. This king is called____ _____ ____ _____.

    23:6

15. The false prophets broke Jeremiah's _____. 23:9-11

16. How many times has Jeremiah told us that God condemns following "the dictates" of our own heart? NKJV

    _____

17. In Jeremiah 23:29, God's word is compared to a _____ and a _____.

18. The "good figs" represent those who would go into _____for their own _____. 24:5

19. The desolation of Judah would last _____ years. 25:11-12

20. What other nations would God punish for their sins? 25:15-25 _____

    _____

Lesson 8

Blessings after Bondage

Jeremiah 26 – 31

In chapter 26, Jeremiah predicted that the glory of the LORD would leave the temple just as it did when the ark was taken from the tabernacle at Shiloh and that Jerusalem would become desolate. In chapters 27 and 28, Jeremiah wore a yoke on his neck symbolizing the submission of Judah and other nations to the Babylonians. However, after seventy years of bondage, blessings would come (chapters 29-31). Those of the true Israel would be restored to God's favor. They would be permitted to return to their homeland; and in the days to come, they would be given a new covenant.

The Yoke of Bondage
Jeremiah 27-28

Chapters 27 and 28 relate events in the reign of Zedekiah, the last king of Judah. Some translations have Jehoiakim as king in 27:1, because most of the Hebrew manuscripts have it that way. However, there is agreement among scholars that "Jehoiakim" reflects a rare scribal error which should be corrected to "Zedekiah". Three Hebrew manuscripts read "Zedekiah" in **27:1**. and the context proves that Zedekiah was the king. (27:3, 12, 20, and 28:1).

The date was about 594 BC—thus shortly after the exile of some 10,000 prominent Jews (2 Kings 24:10-17). The events of chapter 28 were in "the same year" as the events of chapter 27, according to 28:1.

In the beginning of the reign of Zedekiah ... this word came to Jeremiah from the LORD, saying— "Make for yourself bonds and yokes and put it on your neck, and send word (Lit., *them*) *to the king of Edom, to the king of Moab, to the king of the sons of Ammon, to the king of Tyre, and to the king of Sidon by the messengers who come to Jerusalem to Zedekiah king of Judah. And command them to go to their masters, saying, 'Thus says the LORD of hosts the God of Israel ... "I have made the earth, the men and the beasts ... by My great power ... And now I have given all these lands into the hand of Nebuchadnezzar king of Babylon, My servant."* **27:1-6** NASB The yoke would serve as a symbol of the bondage each nation would suffer during the Babylonian rule. (Read Daniel 4:17)

These nations would serve Nebuchadnezzar and the kings of Babylon that followed him. This stern warning was given to the nations meeting in Jerusalem at that time: *"The nation and kingdom which will not serve the same Nebuchadnezzar king of Babylon and will not put their neck under the yoke of the king of Babylon, that nation I will punish,"* says the LORD, *"with the sword, and with the famine and with the pestilence, until I have consumed them by his hand."* **27:8**

The LORD warned the neighboring nations not to listen to their prophets and diviners who were assuring them that they would not serve Babylon. **27:9** He said, *"They prophesy a lie to you, to remove you far from your land; and that I should drive you out, and you should perish."* **27:10** The nation that submitted to Babylon's yoke would remain in their own land. **27:11**

Jeremiah then said to Zedekiah king of Judah, *"Bring your necks under the yoke of the king of Babylon, and serve him and his people and live!"* **27:12** NKJV The king had rebelled against Babylon and refused to pay tribute. He was in serious trouble! Jeremiah warned the king not to listen to the encouraging messages of the false prophets, *"for they prophesy a lie to you."* **27:14** God had not sent them! This message to Zedekiah came in the beginning of Zedekiah's reign.

Jeremiah went with his "yoke message" to the priests and the people. He said, *"Do not listen to the words of your prophets; ... serve the king of Babylon, and live!"* **27:16, 17** NKJV The false prophets were saying the temple vessels that were taken away by the Babylonians during the reigns of Jehoiakim and Jehoiachin would be returned soon to the temple. A true prophet of the LORD would make intercession for the few vessels and treasures that remained in the temple, because the LORD had decreed that *"They shall be carried away to Babylon, and there they shall remain until the day that I visit them. ... Then I will bring them up and restore them to this place."* **27:18-22** NKJV

Later that same year, **the false prophet Hananiah** spoke to Jeremiah in the temple in the presence of the priests and all the people, claiming that he had received a message from the LORD. He announced: *"Thus speaks the LORD of hosts, the God of Israel, saying, 'I have broken the yoke of the king of Babylon.'"* Hananiah falsely testified that God had promised that within two years, he would bring back all the temple vessels, restore Jeconiah (Jehoiachin) as king, and return all the captives from Babylon. **28:1-4**

Jeremiah said to Hananiah, *"Amen! May the LORD do so; may the LORD confirm your words which you have prophesied."* **28:6** NASB Jeremiah was not agreeing with Hananiah; he knew Hananiah's prophecy of peace would not be fulfilled in two years. But Jeremiah did desire the return of the temple vessels and the return of the Jews who had been taken captive to Babylon. **Amen** means "let it be so."

Jeremiah reminded the people how God confirms the word of a prophet. He said, *"The prophet who prophesies of peace, when the word of the prophet shall come to pass, then shall the prophet be known, that the LORD has truly sent him."*

28:7-9 (Deut. 18:22) The yoke of Babylon was not broken within two years. Jehoiachin did not return from Babylon. (Jer. 52:31-34) Hananiah was a false prophet.

Then Hananiah took the yoke off Jeremiah's neck and broke it, saying, *"Thus says the LORD, 'Even so I will break the yoke of Nebuchadnezzar ... within the space of two full years.'"* Hananiah was dramatic! Talk was useless, so Jeremiah left the temple. **28:10-11**

Later, the LORD sent Jeremiah back to Hananiah with a new message: ***"Hear now, Hananiah, the LORD has not sent you, but you make this people trust in a lie. Therefore, thus says the LORD: 'This year you shall die, because you have taught rebellion against the LORD.'"*** So, he died two months later. **28:12-17** God has spoken!

The Hope of Future Blessings
Jeremiah 29 – 31

Jeremiah sent a letter to all the exiles in Babylon. **29:1-2** He wrote this letter after 10,000 Jewish captives were taken from Jerusalem to Babylon in 597 BC (2 Kings 24:14-15). Among the men that king Zedekiah sent to Babylon were **Elasah**, son of Shaphan and **Gemariah**, son of Hilkiah. Another son of Shaphan, Ahikam, had protected Jeremiah when the priests and false prophets tried to kill him. (26:24) Hilkiah was the high priest who found the lost Book of the Law in the time of Josiah's reformation, and Shaphan was the scribe. (2 Kings 22:8) These two men could be trusted to carry Jeremial's letter to the exiles.

Jeremiah wrote: ***"Thus says the LORD of hosts, the God of Israel, to all who are carried away captives, whom I have caused to be carried away from Jerusalem to Babylon."*** **29:4** Their being away from home was not just bad luck.

God encouraged the exiles: ***"Build houses and dwell in them; plant gardens and eat the fruit of them. Take wives and beget sons and daughters."*** **29:5-6**

God would preserve "the remnant" in order to bring the Messiah into the world. The LORD said, ***"And seek the peace of the city where I have caused you to be carried away as captives, and pray to the LORD for it; for in the peace thereof shall you have peace."*** **29:7** If we trust in the LORD, his peace can be with us always. (Philippians 4:4-11)

The LORD warned the exiles not to be deceived by the false prophets among them who were saying that they would return home soon.

This is what the LORD says: "When seventy years are completed for Babylon, I will come to you and fulfill my gracious promise to bring you back to this place. For I know the plans I have for you," declares the LORD, "plans to prosper you and not harm you, plans to give you hope and a future." **29:10-11** ᴺᴵⱽ This promise of hope in the future was fulfilled when the Jews returned from exile and in the new covenant of Christ.

"Then you will call upon Me and go and pray to Me, and I will listen to you. And you will seek Me and find Me when you search for Me with all your heart. I will be found by you," says the LORD, "and I will bring you back from your captivity." **29:12-14** ᴺᴷᴶⱽ

Jeremiah exposed **two false prophets** who were in Babylon—**Ahab** the son of Kolaiah and **Zedekiah** the son of Maaseiah. **29:15-23** They were promising an early return to Jerusalem. They would become a proverbial curse: ***"The LORD make you like Zedekiah and Ahab, whom the king of Babylon roasted in the fire."*** **29:22** They were executed, because they "committed adultery with their neighbors' wives" and had "spoken lying words." **29:22-23**

Shemaiah, another false prophet exiled in Babylon, had sent letters to the priests in Jerusalem, demanding that they put Jeremiah in prison and in the stocks for being a demented false prophet, because he had written to the exiles in Babylon that the captivity would be for a long time. **29:24-29** The LORD told Jeremiah to write to the exiles: ***"Thus says the LORD … 'Because Shemaiah has prophesied to you, and I sent him not, and he caused you to trust in a lie. Behold, I will punish Shemaiah.'"*** **29** He and his family would not live to see the good that the LORD would do for His people, ***"because he has taught rebellion against the LORD."*** **29:31-32**

Hope of Peace in the Future
Jeremiah 30 – 31

Future peace would be realized with the return of both Israel and Judah to their homeland. The ultimate blessing would be the coming of Christ and his new covenant.

The LORD said to Jeremiah, ***"Write all the words that I have spoken to you in a book."*** **30:1** After the Medes and Persians had conquered Babylon, Daniel "understood from the Scriptures, according to the word of the LORD given to Jeremiah that the desolation of Jerusalem would last seventy years." [30] Then Daniel prayed a humble prayer as Jeremiah had given instructions in 29:10-14. [31]

The LORD promised, ***"I will bring again the captivity of my people Israel and Judah … and I will cause them to return to the land that I gave to their fathers, and they shall possess it."*** **30:3** Wayne Jackson makes these comments: "During the restoration following the exile, refugees from both Israel and Judah returned to Palestine. Remember that Babylon had conquered Assyria—where Israel had gone. [32]

---

[30] Daniel 9:1-2, NIV
[31] Daniel 9:3-19
[32] Wayne Jackson, *Jeremiah & Lamentations,* p. 76

"Alas! for that day is great, so that none is like it: it is even the time of Jacob's trouble; but he shall be saved out of it. **30:7** The suffering would be great during the last days before the fall of Jerusalem, but "the just shall live by his faith." (Habakkuk 2:4) *"I will break his yoke from your neck ... and David will be their king."* **30:8,9**

Robert Taylor, Jr. comments: "No longer will they be in exile and under strangers, but to their own land they will return. Under the gospel, God's people will serve the Lord, and David will be their king. This refers to the Messiah—not to Jesse's son who died centuries before." [33]

"Therefore, fear not, O my servant Jacob," says the LORD; "neither be dismayed, O Israel. For, lo, I will save you from afar, and your seed from the land of their captivity; and Jacob shall return and be in rest." **30:10**

God would make *"a full end"* of the Assyrians, the Babylonians, and the Medes & Persians, but he would not make *"a full end"* of Israel. **30:11** A remnant would be saved. (Romans 9:24-27; 11:5) Israel's punishment was for correction. (Hebrews 12:5-11.)

The LORD says to Israel, *"Your wound is incurable."* Then he promises, *"I will restore health to you and heal your wounds."* **30:12-17** [NIV] James Burton Coffman explains: "From the human standpoint there was no remedy for the condition of Israel, but God would supply the healing and restoration which were impossible from any other source." [34] (Ephesians 2:1-10.) Jerusalem will be rebuilt. **30:18-20**

"And their ruler shall come forth from their midst; and I will bring him near, and he shall approach Me; for who would dare to risk his life to approach Me?" declares the LORD. **30:21** [NASB]

---

[33] Robert Taylor, Jr. *Studies in Jeremiah & Lamentations,* Vol. 1, p. 243
[34] James Burton Coffman, *Jeremiah,* Jeremiah 30:12-17, **Bible**soft

Israel's restoration in Jerusalem serves as a type of the church. Christ is the ruler from their midst who would approach God. **30:21.** (Deut. 18:15 and Hebrews 9:11-12.) The LORD will say to the church, the "New Jerusalem" – *"You shall be my people, and I will be your God."* **30:22** (Rev. 21:2-10) *In the latter days*, God's people will understand the purposes of God's heart. **30:24**

"At the same time," says the LORD, "I will be the God of all the families of Israel, and they shall be my people." **31:1** **"At the same time"** refers to the Messianic era, because he mentioned **"the latter days"** in the preceding verse. The blessings would be for those of all the tribes of Israel—not just those of Judah.

The Assyrian and Babylonian captivities are compared with Israel's time in the wilderness, where they survived by God's grace and were promised *rest*. **31:2** The LORD says, *"I have loved you with an everlasting love."* Therefore, the *virgin of Israel* would be restored. **31:3-4** Wayne Jackson explains, "The term *virgin* (which suggests purity) hints that the prophet is speaking of a new kind of Israel—*a spiritual Israel*, not the old, physical nation (cf. 2 Cor. 11:2)." [35]

Watchmen on Mt. Ephraim will cry, *"Arise, and let us go up to Zion, unto the LORD our God,"* … and say, *"O LORD, save your people, the remnant of Israel."* **31:6-7**

After the exile, they returned to earthly Jerusalem. In the gospel of Christ, they shall come to heavenly Zion. (Hebrews 12:22; Rev. 14:1-5) Jerusalem was the physical place of worship before Christ came. He established the church, the spiritual place to worship God "in spirit and truth." (John 4:19-24; Ephesians 3:21)

The LORD says, *"They shall come weeping."* **31:9** They will have godly sorrow that leads to repentance. (2 Cor. 7:10)

[35] Wayne Jackson, *Jeremiah & Lamentations,* p. 80

"He that scattered Israel will gather him, and keep him, as a good shepherd." **31:10** Christ is the good shepherd who gathers his sheep. (John 10:7-16)

Thus says the LORD, "A voice was heard in Ramah, lamentation, and bitter weeping; Rachel, weeping for her children." **31:15** Rachel's grandson Ephraim stands for the kingdom of Israel that was carried away by Assyria. Descendants of her son Benjamin were part of the kingdom of Judah that was in the Babylonian captivity. Matthew 2:17 says that this verse was fulfilled when Herod the Great killed the infants in Bethlehem in an attempt to destroy Jesus. In both cases the temporary suffering was followed by a joyful future. *"Refrain your voice from weeping, and your eyes from tears: for your work shall be rewarded ... your children shall come again to their own border."* **31:16-17** As the Babylonian exile was followed by the return to Jerusalem, so the Bethlehem massacre was followed by the ministry of Christ and salvation by grace.

I have heard Ephraim grieving, "You have disciplined me, and I was disciplined ... bring me back that I may be restored, for you are the LORD my God. **31:18.** Ephraim (Israel) will say, *"I repented ... after I was instructed."* **31:19** The LORD will say, *"I will have mercy upon him."* **31:20** Judah is also included in God's promise of restoration in verses **23-28**.

The LORD promises **a new covenant in Jeremiah 31:31-34.** Israel had broken God's covenant. The new covenant would be with spiritual Israel, including those from other nations. (Galatians 6:15-16) The old covenant was entered into by a physical birth. We enter the new covenant by a new spiritual birth. (John 3:3-5) We become "a new creation" when "baptized into Christ". (2 Cor. 5:17; Rom. 6:3) God's laws ae to be in our mind and heart. (Hebrews 8:7-10)

The LORD promises, *"I will be their God, and they shall be my people"* and *"I will forgive their iniquity, and "I will remember their sin no more."* **31:33, 34** (cf. Hebrews 8:6-12)

God's faithfulness in the order of nature gives assurance that he will not cast off all the seed of Israel. **31:35-37** Wayne Jackson states that "the prophecy deals with the Lord's abiding care for his new nation, spiritual Israel—the church of Jesus Christ (1 Peter 2:9; Galatians 6:16). This is evidenced by the following factors: (1) The context demonstrates that this promise is made to the people who, under the terms of the new covenant, have had their iniquities forgiven (vs. 34), and this is the church. (2) Jesus plainly declared that the reign of God would be taken away from national Israel and given to a "nation" that would produce appropriate fruits, and that the residue of old Israel would be scattered as dust (Matthew 21:43, 44). Just as the heaven above cannot be measured, and the depths of the earth cannot be explored, so God will not cast off "the seed of Israel" (which is the same as Abraham's "seed"—Galatians 3:26-29) for all they have done (37). Why? Because their evil deeds have been forgiven through the blood of Jesus Christ (34)." [36]

"Behold, the days come," says the LORD, *"that the city shall be built to the LORD."* **31:38** The New Jerusalem, the church, is described figuratively in verses **38-40**. (cf. Rev. 21:2-7, 9-19 and Eph. 5:25-32)

---

[36] Wayne Jackson, *Jeremiah & Lamentations*, pp. 86-87

Review Questions on Lesson 8
Jeremiah 26 – 31

1. "_____ after Bondage" is in chapters 26-31.

2. Jeremiah wore a _____ on his neck symbolizing their bondage in Babylon. 27:2

3. After _____ years of bondage, blessings would come.

4. _____ was king of Judah at this time. 27:3, 28:1

5. Ambassadors from the kings of _____, _____, _____, _____, and _____ had come to Jerusalem to form a coalition against Babylon. 27:3

6. Jeremiah commanded the kings of these nations to serve the king of _____ or be consumed with the _____, the _____, and the _____. 27:8

7. The false prophet Hananiah said that within _____ years the LORD would bring back all the temple vessels, restore Jehoiachin as king, and return all the captives.
28:1-4

8. What is the true test of a prophet? 28:9

_____

9. Jeremiah told Hananiah he would die that _____, and he died _____ months later. 28:16, 17 and 28:1

10. In 597 BC, to whom did Jeremiah send a letter? 29:4

_____

11. God told the exiles to build _____,
    plant _____, and take _____. 29:5

12. The promise of hope in the future would be fulfilled
    in the _____ of the Jews from Babylon and
    in the new _____ of Christ. 29:11

13. God said, "You will seek Me and find Me, when you
    search for Me with all your _____." 29:13 ᴺᴷᴶⱽ

14. "O LORD, save your people, the _____ of
    Israel!" 31:7

15. After the LORD sees and hears the repentance of Israel,
    He said, "I will surely have _____ upon him."
    31:16-20

16. In the new covenant, the LORD promises, "I will be
    their _____ and they shall be my _____ . . .
    for I will _____ their iniquity, and
    I will remember their _____ no more." 31:31-34

Lesson 9

Hope during Calamity

Jeremiah 32 – 34

This is the word that came to Jeremiah from the LORD in the tenth year of Zedekiah king of Judah. 32:1 Jerusalem had been under siege by the Babylonians for about a year. The date was 587 BC, and the city would fall in July of the following year. Jeremiah's prophecies against the city were being fulfilled. Zedekiah had put Jeremiah "in the court of the prison" because he did not like Jeremiah's prophecies of defeat. 32:2-5 However, during the calamity of the fall of Jerusalem, there was hope.

Jeremiah Buys a Field
Jeremiah 32:1-15

The LORD revealed to Jeremiah, *"Behold, Hanamel the son of Shallum your uncle shall come to you, saying, 'Buy my field that is in Anathoth, for the right of redemption is yours to buy it.'"* 32:7 The nearest relative had the duty under the law to redeem family land to keep it from being sold outside the family. (Lev. 25-28; Ruth 4:1-12; 1 Kings 21:3) Jeremiah's cousin may have had financial problems that were forcing him to sell the land, or he may have been plotting against Jeremiah (cf. 11:21), testing Jeremiah's sincerity about his hope for the future.

Warren Wiersbe observes: "The field was in the hands of the Babylonians, Jeremiah was in prison, and the future of the nation was bleak indeed. Of what use would a field be to Jeremiah? That, however, is what faith is all about: obeying God in spite of what we see, how we feel, and what may happen. Jeremiah signed the deeds, paid the money and gave the legal documents to his secretary Baruch, who is mentioned here for the first time." [37]

Jeremiah charged Baruch before witnesses to put the sealed purchase deed and the open deed in an earthen vessel to keep and protect them for many days. **32:13-14** (The Dead Sea scrolls were preserved in similar clay jars.)

Jeremiah explains why God wanted him to buy this field, saying, *"For thus says the LORD of hosts, the God of Israel: 'Houses and fields and vineyards shall be possessed again in this land.'"* **32:15** Buying land was a symbolic message of hope that life would return to normal in the future.

Hope during Calamity
Jeremiah 32:16 - 33:13

Jeremiah praises God for his creative power, kindness and justice, as he prays for understanding. *"Lord GOD! Behold, You have made the heavens and the earth by Your great power ... You show lovingkindness to thousands and repay the iniquity of the fathers ... You have caused all this calamity to come upon them. Look, the siege mounds! They have come to the city to take it ... What you have spoken has happened; there You see it! And you have said to me, O Lord GOD, 'Buy the field for money, and take witnesses!'* —yet the city has been given into the hand of the Chaldeans."* **32:16-25** [NKJV] Buying a field at that time did not make any sense. Jeremiah's obedience was a testimony to his faith in God.

The LORD answers Jeremiah's prayer. He begins by asking, *"Is there anything too hard for me?"* **32:27** God's power would be revealed in two ways: first, by his destruction of the city of Jerusalem by the Babylonians (**32:28-36**), and second, by the restoration of his people.

---

[37] Warren W. Wiersbe, *Be Decisive*, pp. 135-136

"Behold, I will gather them out of all countries where I have driven them ... And they shall be my people, and I will be their God. And I will give them one heart, and one way ... And I will make an everlasting covenant with them." **32:37-40**

This everlasting new covenant was promised in Jeremiah 31:31-34; and it was established by Christ through the gospel. (Hebrews 8:6-13; Matthew 26:27-28) The people would have **one heart** (Acts 2:42-46); and there would be **one way** (Ephesians 2:15-16, 4:1-6). Israel would need to be restored to their homeland in order for Christ to come with his new covenant and blessings.

The LORD promised, *"Just as I have brought all this great calamity on this people, so I will bring on them all the good that I have promised them."* **32:41-42** ᴺᴷᴶⱽ After the Babylonian exile, those scattered would return and *buy fields for money, sign deeds and seal them, and take witnesses* as symbolized by Jeremiah's buying a field. **32:43-44** ᴺᴷᴶⱽ

The LORD Promises Health and Healing
Jeremiah 33

While Jeremiah was still shut up in the court of the prison, the LORD said, *"Call to me, and I will answer you, and show you great and mighty things."* **33:3** Although the inhabitants of Jerusalem were preparing to fight against the Chaldeans, the LORD says, *"Behold, I will bring it health and cure, and I will cure them, and reveal to them the abundance of peace and truth."* **33:5-6** The captives of Judah and of Israel would return and rebuild their cities and homes after they repented of their sins and received forgiveness. **33:7-8** The cities of Judah that were "desolate, without man and without beast" would be filled with *the voice of joy and the voice of gladness ... the voice of them that shall say, "Praise the LORD of hosts, for the LORD is good, for his mercy endures forever."* **33:9-11**

Wayne Jackson says, "The return from captivity was a precursor to the glories of the messianic age. The real 'cure' will come from the Great Physician!" [38]

"Behold, the days are coming." **33:14** ᴺᴷᴶⱽ This is a reference to the Christian age. At this time God would perform the good that he had promised to Israel and Judah.

"At that time, I will cause to grow up to David a Branch of righteousness ... In those days Judah will be saved, and Jerusalem will dwell safely. And this is the name by which she will be called:

"THE LORD OUR RIGHTEOUSNESS."

"For thus says the LORD: 'David shall never lack a man to sit upon the throne of the house of Israel.'" **33:15-17** ᴺᴷᴶⱽ This prophecy is fulfilled "in Christ." (Gal. 6:15-16) The New Jerusalem is the bride of Christ (Rev 21:2-10); and Christ's bride is his church (Eph. 5:25-27). She will *dwell safely* in heaven, because the LORD is her righteousness. (Hebrews 12:22) Christ is now reigning on his throne in heaven, and his kingdom will have no end. (Luke 1:32-33; Acts 2:29-36)

"And the Levitical priests shall never lack a man before Me to offer burnt offerings." **33:18** ᴺᴬˢᴮ The Levitical priests would serve in the temple that would be rebuilt in Jerusalem after the exile. However, the offerings of the Levitical priests would not be needed when God made his new covenant. There has been a change in the law and in the priesthood (Hebrews 7:11-12; Psalm 110:1-4). "For it is not possible that the blood of bulls and goats should take away sins." (Hebrews 10:4) "Christ died for our sins according to the Scriptures." He was buried and He rose again the third day. (1 Cor. 15:3-4) "He said, 'I come to do thy will, O God.' He takes away the first, that he may establish the second." (Hebrews 10:9) "We are

---

[38] Wayne Jackson, *Jeremiah & Lamentations,* p. 93; and see Matthew 9:12-13.

sanctified through the offering of the body of Jesus Christ once for all." (Hebrews 10:10) Faithful Christians are "a royal priesthood" serving under Christ our great High Priest. (1 Peter 2:9-10; Hebrews 4:14)

God's promises to David and to Abraham are just as sure as his covenant with the day and night. **33:19-26**

The LORD Warns Zedekiah
Jeremiah 34

The LORD sent Jeremiah with a message of warning to Zedekiah king of Judah during Nebuchadnezzar's siege of Jerusalem. **34:1-7** The cities of Lachish and Azekah were the only other fortified cities left standing. The prophet informed Zedekiah that the LORD had given the city of Jerusalem into the hand of the king of Babylon, and it would be burned with fire. Zedekiah would not be able to escape. He would be captured, and king Nebuchadnezzar would speak to him face to face. However, he would not die by the sword. He would go to Babylon and "die in peace" with an honorable funeral.

King Zedekiah had made a covenant with all the people in Jerusalem to proclaim freedom for the slaves. Everyone was to free his Hebrew slave, both male and female; no one was to hold a fellow Jew in bondage. **34:8-9** NIV They may have thought that freeing all Jewish slaves would cause God to deliver Jerusalem in a miraculous way as He had done in the time of Hezekiah. (Isaiah 36-37) People today still try to bargain with God. At first, the slave owners let their slaves go free. But later, they made their slaves return and serve them. **34:10-11** The covenant they made meant nothing.

Therefore, the word of the LORD came to Jeremiah … "Thus says the LORD, 'I made a covenant with your fathers in the day that I brought them out of the land of Egypt, out of the house of bondage, saying, "At the end of seven years let every man set free his Hebrew brother, who has been sold to him." But your fathers did not obey Me. Then you recently turned and did what was right in My sight—every man proclaiming liberty to his neighbor. Then you turned around and profaned My name, and every one of you brought back his male and female slaves, whom you had set at liberty, and brought them back into subjection.' 34:12-16

God made a covenant with their fathers when he brought them out of Egypt and freed them from their slavery. The covenant required every man to set free his Hebrew slaves during the seventh year of service (Exodus 21:20), but they and their fathers did not do it. God was pleased that everyone freed their slaves during the siege of Jerusalem. **34:15** They were not only obeying their recent covenant but also the covenant that God had made with them at Mount Sinai. By breaking covenants, they were profaning the name of the LORD. His name is not to be taken in vain. (Exodus 20:7) If we do not mean what we say, our words are ungodly and meaningless.

God said, *"You have not obeyed Me in proclaiming liberty ... Behold, I proclaim liberty to you ... to the sword, to pestilence, and to famine! I will deliver you to trouble among all the kingdoms of the earth." 34:17* NKJV "Do not be deceived; God is not mocked: for whatever a man sows, that shall he also reap." (Galatians 6:7)

"And Zedekiah king of Judah and his princes I will give into the hand of their enemies. ... I will make the cities of Judah a desolation without an inhabitant." 34:21-22

Review Questions on Lesson 9
Jeremiah 32 – 34

1. Chapters 32-34 give "_____ _____ _____".

2. These chapters were written when _____ was king of Judah. 32:1

3. The Babylonian army was besieging _____, and Jeremiah was shut up in the _____. 32:2

4. God told Jeremiah to buy a _____ in Anathoth. 32:6-8

5. Why did the LORD want Jeremiah to do this? 32:15

   _____

6. Jeremiah said to the LORD, "Look, the siege _____! … What you have _____ has happened." 32:24 ᴺᴷᴶⱽ

7. The LORD would make "an _____ covenant." 32:40

8. The LORD promised, "Just as I have brought all this great _____ on this people, so I will bring on them all the _____ I have promised them." 32:42

9. While Jeremiah was still in prison, the LORD said to him, "Call to _____ and I will _____ you." 33:1-3

10. What four things did God promise Jerusalem in 33:6?

    _____

11. The desolate cities of Judah would be filled with the voice of _____ and the voice of _____ . 33:10-11

12. "In those days" and "the days are coming" refer to the _____ age.

13. The LORD warned Zedekiah that he would be captured and go to _____, but he would not die by the _____ . 34:1-5

14. What covenant did Zedekiah and his people make, and then they broke it? 34:8-11 _____
_____

15. According to God's covenant with Israel, after a fellow Hebrew slave had served _____ years, he must be set free. (Deut. 15:12) Had their fathers obeyed that commandment? _____ 34:13-14

16. What had Zedekiah and his people done to the name of the LORD? 34:16 _____

17. God would make the cities of Judah a _____ without an _____ . 34:22

Lesson 10

The Fall of Jerusalem

Jeremiah 35 – 39

Chapters 35 and 36 report events that were in the days of Jehoiakim, king of Judah, to illustrate the truthfulness of God's word. It cannot be destroyed!

The Rechabites Obey Their Father
Jeremiah 35

The word which came to Jeremiah from the LORD in the days of Jehoiakim. 35:1 The events of chapter 35 were several years earlier than those in chapters 32-34. Jeremiah is contrasting the people of Judah with the family of Rechab. The Jews were dishonoring the LORD by disobeying His Law, while the Rechabites honored their father by obeying his command. The Rechabites were a clan of nomadic people loyal to their ancestor Jonadab the son of Rechab.

God said to Jeremiah, *"Go to the house of the Rechabites and speak to them, and bring them into the house of the LORD, into one of the chambers and give them wine to drink."* 35:1-2 Jeremiah brought them into the temple and offered them wine to drink. *But they said, "We will drink no wine, for Jonadab the son of Rechab our father commanded us, saying, 'You shall drink no wine, neither you, nor your sons forever.'"* 35:3-6 They had obeyed all that their father had commanded them. 35:7-10 The LORD then instructed Jeremiah to go to the people of Jerusalem and ask them to learn from the example of the Rechabites. 35:13-14 The Rechabites were honoring their earthly father with their obedience to him, but the nation of Judah would not listen to their heavenly father who was speaking to them through his servants the prophets. 35:15-16

Therefore, thus says the LORD God of hosts, the God of Israel, "I will bring on Judah and on all the inhabitants of Jerusalem all the doom that I have pronounced against them; because I have spoken to them but they have not heard, and I have called to them but they have not answered." 35:17

Because the Rechabites had obeyed the commandment of their father Jonadab, God promised that they would always have someone to stand before Him forever. **35:18-19** This family survived the destruction of Jerusalem, and one of its descendants is mentioned in Nehemiah 3:14.

God's Word Cannot Be Destroyed
Jeremiah 36

In the fourth year of Jehoiakim ... this word came to Jeremiah from the LORD, saying, "Take a scroll of a book, and write therein all the words I have spoken to you against Israel and against Judah, and against all the nations ... from the days of Josiah, even unto this day." 36:1-2 We learn from Jeremiah 25:1-3 that from the beginning of Jeremiah's prophecies in the days of Josiah to the fourth year of Jehoiakim was a period of twenty-three years. Jeremiah needed divine inspiration to enable him to recall these messages that he recorded in the first 25 chapters of his book. The written word of God would be a constant and permanent reminder to the people of the approaching calamity that God had purposed to bring upon them and an incentive for them to repent so God could forgive them. **36:3** The LORD gave these instructions to Jeremiah in the year 605 BC.

Then Jeremiah called Baruch the son of Neriah; and Baruch wrote from the mouth of Jeremiah all the words of the LORD, which he had spoken to him upon a scroll of a book." 36:4 Jeremiah dictated the messages to his secretary Baruch, who wrote down all the words on a scroll. **36:4**

When the writing was completed, Baruch went to the temple and read these words from the scroll in the ears of all Judah on an appointed day of fasting. Jeremiah could not go to the temple himself. **36:5-8**

In the fifth year of Jehoiakim ... in the ninth month ... they proclaimed a fast before the LORD to all the people in Jerusalem and to all the people that came from the cities of Judah to Jerusalem. Then Baruch read in the book the words of Jeremiah in the house of the LORD. **36:9-10** The year was now 604 BC. Baruch probably needed several months to write down Jeremiah's first twenty-five chapters. Also, they had to wait for the next day of fasting.

When Micaiah the son of Gemariah, the son of Shaphan, had heard out of the book all the words of the LORD, he went down into the king's house, into the scribe's chamber. **36:11-12.** Micaiah, a grandson of Shaphan, appears to be Jeremiah's friend, because early in Jehoiakim's reign, Ahikam the son of Shaphan had protected Jeremiah. (26:1, 24) Shaphan had been the scribe of good king Josiah. (2 Kings 22:3) Micaiah told the king's officials all the words that he had heard when Baruch read the scroll. **36:13** Therefore, they brought in Baruch to read the scroll to them. When they had heard these written words, they were afraid and said that they would have to tell these words to the king. **36:15-16**

After questioning Baruch as to how he came to write the scroll, the officials told Baruch that he and Jeremiah should hide themselves, and let no one know where they were. **36:17-19** They were protecting Jeremiah and his scribe from the anticipated rage of the king upon hearing Jeremiah's words. They feared that King Jehoiakim might order the prophet's death. (cf. 26:20-23). They probably recognized that the scroll had to have been written by the inspiration of God. For this reason, these officials had saved Jeremiah's life before in the early days of Jehoiakim. (26:1-16)

After putting the scroll in the chamber of Elishama the scribe, the officials reported to the king all that they had just heard. **36:20** King Jehoiakim ordered Jehudi to bring the scroll and read it to him and to all the officials that stood beside him. **36:21**

Now the king sat in the winter house in the ninth month; and there was a fire on the hearth burning before him. **36:22** The ninth month would be in our November and December. When Jehudi had read three or four columns of the scroll, the king fearlessly *cut it with a penknife and cast it into the fire that was on the hearth, until all the scroll was consumed in the fire.* **36:23-24** Jehoiakim thought he could destroy the power of God's word by burning it with fire. As he was destroying the scroll, three of his officials (princes) pleaded with him not to do it; but he would not listen. **36:25** (36:12) Jehoiakim ordered the arrest of Baruch the scribe and Jeremiah the prophet; but the LORD had hidden them. **36:26**

Then the word of the LORD came to Jeremiah, saying, "Take again another scroll and write in it all the former words that were in the first scroll, which Jehoiakim the king of Judah burned." **36:27-28** He instructed Jeremiah to tell Jehoiakim that the king of Babylon would certainly come and destroy their land. Jehoiakim would have none of his sons to sit on the throne of David in Jerusalem, because his son Jehoiachin reigned only three months before he was taken captive to Babylon (2 Kings 24:6-12). Jehoiakim's dead body would be cast out and exposed to the heat and cold. **36:29-31**

Then Jeremiah took another scroll and gave it to Baruch the scribe ... who wrote therein from the mouth of Jeremiah all the words of the book which Jehoiakim king of Judah had burned in the fire; and there were add besides to them many like words." **36:32** The LORD's word cannot be destroyed. God has spoken!

And King Zedekiah the son of Josiah reigned instead of Coniah the son of Jehoiakim, whom Nebuchadnezzar king of Babylon made king in the land of Judah. But neither he, nor his servants, nor the people listened to the words of the LORD. **37:1-2**

Since the last two chapters were during Jehoiakim's reign, we are reminded that Zedekiah was placed on the throne by Nebuchadnezzar king of Babylon after the three-months reign of Coniah (Jehoiachin) the son of Jehoiakim. (2 Kings 24:8,17) Zedekiah and the people refused to hear Jeremiah's warnings that they should surrender to the Babylonians to save their city. The last days of the siege are reported in chapters 37 and 38, and the fall of Jerusalem is in chapter 39.

Zedekiah's False Hope
Jeremiah 37:1-10

Zedekiah sent messengers to Jeremiah, saying, *"Pray now to the LORD our God for us."* **37:3-4** Jeremiah was not in prison at this time. Chapter 37 is describing events before chapter 32 and explains how Jeremiah came to be "shut up in the court of the prison." (32:2) The army of the Chaldeans (Babylonians) left its siege of Jerusalem to deal with the Egyptian army that was coming to Judah's aid. **37:5** Although Zedekiah would not heed Jeremiah's warnings, he could see that Jeremiah's predictions were coming true. He no doubt was hoping that the Babylonian army's departure was a sign that the LORD would save the city, and was requesting Jeremiah to pray for their deliverance.

The LORD instructed Jeremiah to tell the king, *"Behold, Pharaoh's army, which is come forth to help you, shall return to Egypt … And the Chaldeans shall come again and fight against this city … and burn it with fire. Do not deceive yourselves, saying, 'The Chaldeans shall surely depart from us,' for they shall not depart."* **37:6-10**

Jeremiah's Imprisonment
Jeremiah 37:11-21

The lull in the siege gave Jeremiah an opportunity to go home to Anathoth to take care of some family business, but he was seized at one of the gates of Jerusalem and accused of defecting to the enemy. The guard that arrested him was Irijah, a grandson of the false prophet Hananiah, who had mocked Jeremiah in chapter 28. The officials before whom Jeremiah was brought were not the same ones who had defended him earlier in 26:10-16, because they were carried away into Babylon along with Jehoiachin in 597 BC, according to 2 Kings 24:12, 15. The new group of officials beat Jeremiah and put him in a dungeon prison in Jonathan's house for many days. **37:11-16**

Then Zedekiah the king sent and took him out; and the king asked him, "Is there any word from the LORD?" And Jeremiah said, "There is ... You shall be delivered into the hand of king of Babylon." 37:17

Jeremiah asked the king why he had been put in prison. The false prophets should be the ones in prison. He said to the king, *"Where are now your prophets who prophesied to you, saying, 'The king of Babylon shall not come against you, nor against this land?'" 37:18-19* Jeremiah had warned the king about everything that had happened. So, he begged the king, *"Cause me not to return to the house of Jonathan the scribe, lest I die there."* Then Zedekiah ordered that he be placed in *"the court of the prison"*—a place for privileged prisoners— and that he should receive a piece of bread each day. **37:20-21**

Jeremiah's Rescue from Death
Jeremiah 38:1-13

While in the court of the prison, Jeremiah was able to warn the people about staying in the city and to encourage them to surrender to the Babylonians. (Jer. 32-33) Three princes urged the king to put Jeremiah to death because he was discouraging the war effort. The power of the princes and the weakness of Zedekiah are seen in his response. *Then Zedekiah the king said, "Behold, he is in your hand: for the king is not he that can do anything against you." Then they took Jeremiah and cast him into the dungeon ... that was in the court of the prison.* **38:1-6**

The "dungeon" into which Jeremiah was let down by ropes appears to be an old cistern where *there was no water, but mire*. As Jeremiah was left to die in the darkness and in the mud, surely his words of despair returned to his mind. (cf. 20:14-18) *"Out of the depths I have cried unto you, O LORD."* (Psalm 130:1) The LORD used an Ethiopian eunuch that was in the king's house to answer Jeremiah's prayers. (cf. Acts 8:26-39) Ebed-Melech pleaded Jeremiah's case before the king, and Zedekiah commanded that he be lifted out of the pit so he would not die. Jeremiah was returned to the court of the prison. **38:7-13**

Jeremiah's Last Warning to Zedekiah
Jeremiah 38:14-28

Zedekiah the king arranged for a private meeting with Jeremiah at the temple and swore secretly to protect Jeremiah if he would give him information from the LORD and "hide nothing." The message to Zedekiah was this: *"If you will surrender to the officials of the king of Babylon, then your life shall be spared, and this city shall not be burned with fire, and you and your house shall live."* **38:17** ᴱˢⱽ Even at this late date, if Zedekiah would listen to the LORD, the city of Jerusalem would be spared and his entire family would survive. But the king was afraid of what the Jewish exiles in Babylon might do to him. Jeremiah assured him, *"Obey, I beseech you, the voice of the LORD, which I speak to you; so it shall be well to you, and your soul shall live."* **38:20** However, if he refused to surrender, he would be responsible for Jerusalem being burned with fire. Instead of obeying the LORD, he was concerned about what his political advisors would think of him. If the princes should question Jeremiah about his visit with the king, he was to tell them that he was making his request not to be sent back to the dungeon in Jonathan's house to die. This answer satisfied the princes, and Jeremiah remained in the court of the prison until the fall of Jerusalem. **38:21-28**

The Fall of Jerusalem
Jeremiah 39:1-11

In the ninth year of Zedekiah king of Judah, in the tenth month, Nebuchadnezzar king of Babylon and all his army came against Jerusalem, and they besieged it." **39:1** This siege lasted for one and a half years. The city finally fell in July, 586 BC, in the eleventh year, the fourth month of Zedekiah's reign. **39:2**

The Babylonian officials entered the city and set up their command post at the Middle Gate. **39:3** Zedekiah and his family with his bodyguards and nobles tried to escape by night, but the Babylonians captured them and brought them to Nebuchadnezzar at his headquarters in Riblah, Syria, about 200 miles north of Jerusalem. The last thing Zedekiah would remember seeing before his eyes were put out was the sight of his sons being killed. Nebuchadnezzar also killed all the nobles of Judah. Zedekiah was bound and taken to Babylon just as Jeremiah had predicted. **39:4-7**

All of the personal loss suffered by Zedekiah could have been avoided if only he had obeyed the LORD. Back in Jerusalem, the walls were broken down, and the king's palace and all the houses were burned with fire, including the temple. (52:13) Those who had survived in Jerusalem along with those who had defected were carried away to Babylon, except for the poor people who were to take care of the vineyards and the fields. **39:8-10**

Jeremiah Is Set Free
Jeremiah 39:11-18

Nebuchadnezzar instructed Nebuzaradan the captain of the Babylonian guard to protect Jeremiah. The king must have known that Jeremiah had been encouraging his people to surrender. Jeremiah was taken from the court of the prison and placed under the care of Gedaliah the son of Ahikam, who had protected Jeremiah earlier. (26:24) Jeremiah remained in Judah with the remnant of the poor people. **39:11-14**

Before the fall of Jerusalem, the LORD sent Jeremiah to the Ethiopian, Ebed-Melech, promising that he would not be killed or captured. He would live because he had saved Jeremiah's life by putting his trust in the LORD. **39:15-18**

Review Questions on Lesson 10
Jeremiah 35 – 39

1. The LORD blessed the family of the _____,
   because for over 250 years they had obeyed their father
   by not drinking any wine? 35:1-19

2. Why was God bringing doom on Judah and Jerusalem?
   35:15-17 _____

3. Who tried to destroy God's word by burning it? 36:1-23

   _____

4. The scribe named _____ wrote down on a scroll
   the messages of the LORD from the mouth of Jeremiah.
   36:32

5. What did Zedekiah king of Judah want Jeremiah to do?
   37:3 _____

6. At this time what was the Babylonian army doing? 37:5

   _____

7. What happened to Jeremiah when he tried to go into the
   land of Benjamin at this time? (37:11-14)

   _____

8. What did the princes do to Jeremiah? 37:15

   _____

9. Who brought Jeremiah to the palace and put him in the
   court of the prison? 37:17-21 _____

10. Three princes put Jeremiah in a _____ hoping he would die there? 38:1-6

11. Who was responsible for the rescue of Jeremiah?

    38:7-13 _____
    How did God reward this man? 39:15-18

    _____

12. What did the LORD promise Zedekiah if he would surrender to Babylon? 38:17 _____

    _____

13. What was Zedekiah afraid of? 38:19

    _____

    _____

14. When did the city of Jerusalem fall? 39:1-2

    _____

15. When the king tried to escape, he was captured and brought to Nebuchadnezzar's headquarters that were in _____, _____. 39:4-5

16. What did Zedekiah see before his eyes were put out? 39:6-7

    _____

17. The poor were left to care for _____ and _____. 39:10

18. Jeremiah was taken out of prison and placed under the care of_____ the son of _____. 39:11-14

NOTES

Lesson 11

After the Fall of Jerusalem

Jeremiah 40 – 46

Jeremiah with Governor Gedaliah
Jeremiah 40:1-12

Although Nebuzaradan, commander of the Babylonian guard, had released Jeremiah from the court of the prison to be with his people (39:11-14), Jeremiah somehow got mixed up with the captives at Ramah that were being made ready to go to Babylon. When Nebuzaradan discovered that Jeremiah was among the captives, he removed his chains and gave the prophet a choice. He could either go to Babylon where he would be treated well or stay with Gedaliah, whom the king of Babylon had made governor over the cities of Judah, and live with the poor of his people. Realizing that they needed him, Jeremiah chose to remain with his people. Before letting him go, the captain gave him food and a gift. **40:1-5**

Then Jeremiah went to Gedaliah the son of Ahikam Mizpah and dwelt with him among the people that were left in the land. **40:6** Gedaliah was of the godly family of Ahikam, the son of Shaphan. Those who were hiding and those who had fled to other countries returned to Judah, because of their confidence in Gedaliah. He encouraged them to serve the king of Babylon. **40:7-12** Mizpah was eight miles north of Jerusalem. Samuel had judged Israel from Mizpah, which is also spelled Mizpeh. (1 Samuel 7:5)

Johanan Becomes the New Leader
Jeremiah 40:13 – 41:18

Johanan and other former military captains in Judah warned Gedaliah that the king of the Ammonites had sent

Ishmael to murder him. But Gedaliah did not believe them. "In the seventh month" (September – October), Ishmael and ten of his men came to visit Gedaliah at Mizpah.

While eating together, Ishmael and his men killed the governor along with the Jews and Babylonian soldiers that were with him. Ishmael was a descendant of David, and he may have felt that he should have been made the ruler of the nation because of his royal blood, or he may have been motivated simply by greed. **41:1-3**

The next day, Ishmael killed seventy men from Shechem, Shiloh, and Samaria who were on their way to the ruined temple site in Jerusalem with offerings. He then forced the rest of the people in Mizpah, including the king's daughters, to go with him as captives unto Ammon, where he would be rewarded. Jeremiah was probably among the captives; he was living in Mizpah. **41:4-10** When Johanan and the other army officers heard what Ishamel had done, they and their men chased after him and overtook him at the great pool of Gibeon. **41:11-12** All the captives escaped and joined Johanan, while Ishmael fled to Ammon with eight of his men. Johanan and his captains decided to take the people to Egypt, because they feared the wrath that might come when the king learned of Gedaliah's death. **41:13-18**

Flight to Egypt is Forbidden
Jeremiah 42

Johanan and all the people asked Jeremiah to pray *"that the LORD your God may show us the way wherein we may walk and the thing that we may do."* **42:1-3** Their request revealed how far their hearts were away from God. They did not say, "the LORD **our** God", but "**your** God." In his answer, Jeremiah corrected this when he said, *"I will pray to the LORD your God ... and it shall come to pass that whatever thing the LORD shall answer you, I will declare it to you."* **42:4** They promised, *"The LORD be a true and faithful witness between us, if we do not even according to all things for the which the LORD your God shall send you to us."* **42:5** They did not notice his subtle rebuke.

After ten days ... the word of the LORD came to Jeremiah. **42:7** The people wanted to go to Egypt, and they were likely growing impatient. Jeremiah called all the people and told them that the LORD promised. *"If you will stay in this land, I will build you up and not tear you down. ... Do not be afraid of the king of Babylon, whom you now fear. Do not be afraid of him,"* declares the LORD, *"for I am with you and will save you and deliver you from his hands."* **42:10-12** NIV

However, the LORD warned, *"But if you say, 'We will not dwell in this land ... but we will go into the land of Egypt, where we shall see no war' ... then it shall come to pass that the sword, which you feared, shall overtake you there in the land of Egypt, ... and there you shall die."* **42:13-16** Nebuchadnezzar would also conquer the land of Egypt.

Jeremiah warned them, saying, *"Do not go to Egypt! Know certainly that I have admonished you this day. For you were hypocrites in your hearts when you sent me to the LORD."* **42:19-20** NKJV The people didn't want God's plans; they wanted the LORD to approve what they had already decided to do. This should be a warning to us not to be insincere as we seek the will of God.

"Now therefore know certainly that you shall die by the sword, by the famine, and by the pestilence in the place where you desire to go and to sojourn." **42:22**

Jeremiah Is Taken to Egypt
Jeremiah 43

The people had proof that Jeremiah was God's prophet; all that he had said about the fall of Jerusalem was true. Yet they still refused to obey his warning. Johanan and all the people accused him of lying. They said God had not sent him, but he had been influenced by Baruch to say these things. **43:1-3**

"So, they came into the land of Egypt, for they obeyed not the voice of the LORD. Thus, they came even to Tahpanhes." **43:7**

The LORD instructed Jeremiah to bury some large stones in the courtyard at the entrance to the palace of Pharaoh in Tahpanhes. While all the Jews were watching, Jeremiah told them God would bring Nebuchadnezzar to Egypt where he would set his throne above those stones and would burn with fire the temples of the gods of Egypt. **43:8-13**

The LORD reminded the people of the calamity he had brought on Jerusalem because of their wickedness and idolatry. God had sent his servants the prophets to warn them, but they did not listen. Now they were practicing the same sinful things in Egypt. Therefore, the LORD said, *"I will set my face against you for catastrophe and for the cutting off all Judah."* **44:11** NKJV

The people would not listen to the words spoken "in the name of the LORD." Instead, they burned incense to the Queen of Heaven, a fertility goddess. **44:17-19** (cf. 7:18) God answered, *"I have sworn by my great name, that my name shall no more be named in the mouth of any man of Judah in all the land of Egypt."* **44:26** They could never call on his name for help. Then God promised that *"a small number ... shall return out of the land of Egypt into the land of Judah."* **44:28** A remnant would return to Jerusalem after Cyrus issued the decree for the rebuilding of the temple in Jerusalem. (Ezra 1:1-4) Those who stayed in Egypt would know that God's words are true when the Babylonians defeated Pharaoh Hopha. **44:29-30**

Assurance to Baruch
Jeremiah 45

The date is 605 BC, in the fourth year of Jehoiakim's reign. **45:1** Baruch, the faithful scribe, had written down on a scroll the words of Jeremiah. (36:1-6) But, Jehoiakim had burned this scroll and had threatened to kill Baruch. (36:16-26) Baruch had said, *"Woe is me now! For the LORD has added grief to my sorrow."* **45:3** God's message against Jerusalem had caused him sorrow, and now he feared for his own life! The LORD's message to Baruch was: *"Behold, that which I have built I will break down, and that which I have planted I will pluck up, even this whole land."* **45:4** God's judgments against Israel, Judah, and all the nations had been written down by Baruch. (36:2) The LORD told Baruch not to seek great things for himself, but he would give him his *"life as a prize."* **45:5** ᴱˢⱽ

Judgment Against Egypt
Jeremiah 46:1-26

Nebuchadnezzar king of Babylon defeated the Egyptian army in the battle of Carchemish in 605 BC, the fourth year of Jehoiakim. This judgment upon Egypt is called *the day of the Lord GOD of hosts, a day of vengeance.* **46:10** Pharaoh Necho had killed Judah's good king Josiah four years earlier (609 BC) in the battle of Megiddo. Egypt's wound would be incurable. **46:11** The armies of Nebuchadnezzar king of Babylon would invade the land of Egypt and subdue it. **46:13-26**

Israel Will Be Preserved
Jeremiah 46:27-28

The LORD promises his people, *"I will save you from afar off, and your seed from the land of their captivity; and Jacob shall return ... I will not make a full end of you, but will correct you in measure; yet I will not leave you wholly unpunished."* **46:27-28**

NOTES

Review Questions on Lesson 11
Jeremiah 40 – 46

1. Who was made governor of the cities of Judah? 40:5

   _____

2. Who warned Gedaliah of a plot to kill him? 40:13-15

   _____

3. Who killed Gedaliah and those with him at a dinner?
   41:1-3 _____

4. What did Johanan and the people promise when they
   asked Jeremiah to pray to the LORD about their going
   to Egypt? 42:6 _____

   _____

5. What did the LORD say would happen if they went to
   Egypt? 42: 15-16 _____

   _____

6. Jeremiah said, "Know certainly that I have admonished
   you this day. For you were _____ in your
   hearts when you sent me to the Lord your God, saying,
   'Pray for us.' " 42:19-20

7. Johanan and the people accuse Jeremiah of speaking
   _____ . 43:2

8. So they came to the land of _____ for they did
   not _____ the voice of the LORD. 43:7

9. They provoked the LORD to wrath, "burning incense to
   _____ _____ in the land of _____." 44:8

10. In what three ways did God punish the disobedient Jews in Egypt? 44:13 _____

11. What did the people say to Jeremiah in 44:16?

    _____

12. God promised Baruch his _____ as a prize. 45:5

13. The judgment upon Egypt is called "the _____ of the Lord GOD of host." 46:10

14. Nebuchadnezzar king of Babylon defeated the army of Egypt at _____ by the _____ river in _____ BC. 46:2

15. "But do not _____, O My servant Jacob,
    And do not be _____, O Israel!
    For behold, I will _____ you from afar." 46:27
    (Read Romans 9:6)

Lesson 12

God Judges the Nations

Jeremiah 47 – 52

Judgment Against Philistia
Jeremiah 47

Thus says the LORD, "Behold, waters rise out of the north, and shall be an overflowing flood; they shall overflow the land and all that is in it … For the LORD shall plunder the Philistines, the remnant of the country of Caphtor. **47:2, 4** ^{NKJV}

The Philistines came to Palestine from Crete, that is called Caphtor in chapter 47:4. They were a wealthy nation with merchant ships that sailed on the Mediterranean and acquired goods from many lands. They did not have a central government, but were made up of five city states—Gaza, Ashdod, Ashkelon, Gath, and Ekron. (1 Samuel 6:17) The Philistines had the best weapons due to their skilled iron-makers, and they were always a threat to Israel.

The Philistines would fear the Babylonian army that would come from the north like a raging flood that destroys everything. Fathers will flee for their lives forgetting they have children left behind. **47:3** People will beg the LORD to put up his terrible sword of judgment. But this sword would continue to destroy until it had accomplished God's purpose. **47:6-7**

Judgment Against Moab
Jeremiah 48

Against Moab thus says the LORD of hosts the God of Israel … "Because you have trusted in your works and in your treasures, you also shall be taken; and Chemosh shall go forth into captivity with his priests." **48:1-7**

The Moabites were descendants of Lot (Genesis 19:30-37), and their land was southeast of the Dead Sea. There were bad feelings between the Moabites and the Israelites. When the nation Israel tried to enter Canaan, the king of Moab hired Balaam to curse them. (Numbers 22:24)

Warren Wiersbe says, "In 582 BC, Nebuchadnezzar's army invaded Moab, destroyed the people and the cities, and left desolation behind. The reason for this judgment was Moab's pride (48:7, 29-30) and complacency (v. 11). The Moabites were certain that their god Chemosh would protect them (vv. 7, 13, 35, 46)." [39]

"And Moab shall be destroyed from being a people, because he magnified himself against the LORD." **48:42** *"Woe be unto you, O Moab! The people of Chemosh perishes, for your sons are taken captives."* **48:46** The Moabites were absorbed by the Arabs and other surrounding nations. However, the LORD promises, *"Yet I will bring again the captivity of Moab in the latter days."* **48:47** This is a messianic prophecy. Arabs were among those present on Pentecost that heard and obeyed the gospel of Christ. (Acts 2:11, 37-38, 41)

Judgment Against Ammon
Jeremiah 49:1-6

Concerning the Ammonites, thus says the LORD, "Has Israel no sons? Has he no heir? Why then does their king inherit Gad, and his people dwell in his cities? Therefore behold, the days come," says the LORD, "that I will cause an alarm of war to be heard in Rabbah of the Ammonites; and it shall be a desolate heap. Then shall Israel be heir to them that were his heirs," says the LORD. **49:1-2**

---

[39] Warren W. Wiersbe, *Be Decisive*, p. 167

The Ammonites also were descendants of Lot (Genesis 19:38). The land of Ammon was north of Moab and east of the Jordan River, where the modern-day nation of Jordan exists with its capital city of Amman. Ammon was known for its idolatry and especially for its worship of Molech, which involved human sacrifices.[40] Molech's name means "king." It is also written Molock, Milcom, and Malcam. [41]

In 1 Samuel 11, the Ammonites came up against the city of Jabesh Gilead in the tribe of Gad, threating to make them their slaves by putting out their right eyes. However, king Saul of Israel came to their rescue. Years later, when Assyria conquered Gad and along with the other northern tribes of Israel, Ammon quickly invaded and took Gad's territory. They had no inheritance right. Judah was closer related to Israel than Ammon. Judah was the rightful heir.

Because of its sins, their capital city, **Rabbah**, *"shall be a desolate mound, and her villages shall be burned with fire. Then Israel shall take possession of his inheritance."* **49:2** NKJV God's people would return to their land by the proclamation of Cyrus king of Persia after the Babylonian exile. (Ezra 1:1-3) The promise of the LORD to *"bring again the captivity of the people of Ammon"* (**49:6**) is fulfilled in their acceptance of the gospel of Christ. (Luke 4:18-19)

Judgment against Edom
Jeremiah 49:7-22

Concerning Edom. Thus says the LORD of hosts, "Is wisdom no more in Teman … Though you make your nest as high as the eagle's, I will bring you down from there," declares the LORD. And Edom will become an object of horror; everyone who passes by will be horrified and hiss at all its wounds … no one will live there." **49:7,16-18** NASB The

---

[40] 1 Kings 11:5; 2 Kings 23:10; Lev. 20:2
[41] F. N. Peloubet, *Peloubet's Bible Dictionary,* pp. 416, 417

Edomites were descendants of Esau, and the hostility he had against his brother Jacob continued against Israel. Edom denied passage of the Israelites on their way to Canaan during the time of Moses. (Numbers 20:14-21) Edom had rejoiced over the destruction of Jerusalem. (Psalm 137:7)

The men of Teman in Edom were known for their great wisdom (Job 4:1), but they would not be able to devise any plan that would save them. The LORD would make Edom bare like a harvest where nothing is left for the gleaners. **49:8-10** Like the kingdom of Judah, Edom would have to "drink of the cup" of God's wrath. **49:12** The pride of Edom would bring her down. With her cities in the cliffs of the rocks, such as Petra, they would be destroyed because of her pride and rebellion against the LORD.

Judgment against Damascus
Jeremiah 49:23-27

Damascus has grown feeble. She turns to flee, and fear has seized her, ... her young men shall fall in the streets and all the men of war shall be cut off in that day," says the LORD of hosts. **49:24-26** ᴺᴷᴶⱽ Damascus was the capital city of Syria. Amos had accused Damascus of threshing the people of Gilead with instruments of iron. (Amos 1:3) God would judge them for their inhumanity and brutality. The cities of Hamath and Arpad, in northern Syria, would be confounded and fainthearted when they heard what the Babylonians had done to Damascus. Ben-Hadad was a title given to the rulers of Syria. **49:27**

Judgment Against Kedar and Hazor
Jeremiah 49:28-33

Concerning Kedar and the kingdoms of Hazor, which Nebuchadnezzar king of Babylon defeated. Thus says the LORD, "Arise, go up to Kedar and devastate the men of the east." **49:28** *"Run away, flee! Dwell in the depths, O inhabitants of Hazor.* **49:30** ^{NASB} These were two nomadic nations that raised sheep and camels. Those of Kedar were descendants of Ishmael's son by that name. (Genesis 25:13). The identity of Hazor is uncertain. These "wealthy nations" lost everything, when Nebuchadnezzar king of Babylon attacked them in 599-598 BC.

Judgment Against Elam
Jeremiah 49:34-39

Thus says the LORD of hosts, "Behold, I will break the bow of Elam." **49:35** This word against Elam came in the beginning of the reign of Zedekiah (597 BC). **49:34** Ancient Elam was in what is now Iran. Elam was east of the city of Babylon. North and east of Elam was the kingdom of Media; Persia was to the southeast. The original Elamites were descendants of Elam, the oldest son of Shem. (Gen. 10:22) Elam was one of the world's oldest kingdoms. (Gen 14:1)

About 900 BC two Indo-European groups, the Medes and Persians, migrated into the region of Elam. The Medes established a strong state, controlling the Elamites and the Persians. Cyrus the Persian overthrew the Medes and founded the Persian Empire, about 550 BC. [42] From then on, the names of Elam and Persia were used interchangeably.

Elam was known for its skilled archers that were used against Jerusalem. (Isaiah 22:6) The Medes who were ruling in Elam at the time of Jeremiah's prophecy would lose their power to the Persians.

"And upon Elam I will bring the four winds … of heaven and will scatter them toward all those winds; and there shall be no nation where the outcasts of Elam shall not come." **49:36** The four winds of heaven are used in Daniel 7:2-7 to symbolize the rise and fall of great kingdoms. The Persian

[42] Addison-Wesley, *World History Traditions and New Directions,* p. 42

Empire would come to power and spread in all directions, according to Daniel 8:1-4, 20.

"And I will set my throne in Elam and will destroy from there the king and the princes," says the LORD. **49:38** This is the key verse of the prophecy. The LORD would show his sovereign power in Elam. Cyrus the Persian established his throne in Elam; and he would be God's instrument over the nations.

In **Isaiah 44:28**, the LORD calls Cyrus "my shepherd" and says, "He shall perform all my pleasure, even saying to Jerusalem, 'You shall be built' and to the temple, 'Your foundation shall be laid.'" Cyrus is "his anointed ... to subdue nations" in **Isaiah 45:1**. The LORD promises that Cyrus "shall build my city, and he shall let go my captives." (Isaiah 45:13) Cyrus first conquered Elam and Media before overthrowing the Babylonian Empire in 539 BC and restoring the Jews to their homeland in Judah in 536 BC.

God promises, *"But it shall come to pass in the latter days that I will bring again the captivity of Elam."* **49:39** This is predicting the time of the Messiah, the Christian age. Elamites were present on Pentecost to hear the gospel and to be added to God's eternal kingdom. (Acts 2:8-9, 36-41, 47)

Judgment Against Babylon
Jeremiah 50 – 51

"The word that the LORD spoke against Babylon" covers two chapters. Babylon had been used as God's instrument to punish Judah and other nations. In Jeremiah 25:9, the LORD called Nebuchadnezzar *"my servant."* But according to 25:12, Babylon would not escape God's judgment for her own sins.

"Declare and proclaim among the nations ... say, 'Babylon has been captured. Bel has been put to shame, Marduk has been shattered; her images have been put to shame, her idols have been shattered.'" **50:2** ᴺᴬˢᴮ The LORD

declared war on Babylon and its many gods. Her chief god was Bel, also called Marduk. Their idols would be powerless, broken, and humiliated—even unable to save themselves. *"For out of the north there comes up a nation against her, which shall make her land desolate."* **50:3** Cyrus's army would invade Babylon from the north, and this would be the beginning of the city of Babylon's decline that ultimately would leave her desolate and uninhabited.

In those days ... the children of Israel shall come, they and the children of Judah together, going and weeping. ... They shall go and seek the LORD their God. They shall ask the way to Zion ... saying, "Come, and let us join ourselves to the LORD in a perpetual covenant that shall not be forgotten." **50:4-5** The return of Israel and Judah to Jerusalem following the fall of Babylon led the way for their coming together under the new covenant of Christ. (Jeremiah 31:31-34)

God says, *"My people have been lost sheep. Their shepherds have caused them to go astray."* **50:6** Their wicked kings, false prophets and ungodly priests were the guilty shepherds. Israel was like sheep scattered first by the king of Assyria and then by the king of Babylon. **50:17** Now it's Babylon's turn to be punished.

Therefore thus says the LORD of hosts, the God of Israel: "Behold, I will punish the king of Babylon and his land, as I have punished the king of Assyria. But I will bring back Israel to his home. ... For I will pardon those whom I preserve." **50:18-20** NKJV Pride was Babylon's greatest sin. *For she has been proud against the LORD, against the Holy One of Israel.* **50:29**

God has the right to judge the nations. *He has made the earth by his power; he has established the world by his wisdom, and has stretched out the heavens by his understanding.* **51:15** He says to a nation, *"You are my battle axe and weapons of war: for with you I will break in pieces* *the nations, and with you I will destroy kingdoms."* **51:20** Babylon had been God's weapon of war against wicked nations. Babylon's time to be punished will come. Babylon will be broken and destroyed by the Medes & Persians. *"The broad walls of Babylon shall be utterly broken, and her high gates shall be burned with fire."* **51:58**

Jeremiah wrote this prophecy during the fourth year of Zedekiah's reign. **51:59** He gave the scroll of this prophecy against Babylon to Baruch's brother Seraiah to read in Babylon, and then he was to throw it into the Euphrates River. (**51:60-64**) This would symbolize the complete destruction of Babylon. After reading the words of this scroll in the city of Babylon, Seraiah tied a stone to the scroll and threw it into the Euphrates River. Then he said, *"Thus, Babylon shall sink and shall not rise from the evil that I will bring upon her."* **51:64a**

Thus far are the words of Jeremiah. **51:64b** This indicates that the last chapter was added by another inspired scribe who gives an historical epilogue to the book.

The Fall of Jerusalem Reviewed
Jeremiah 52:1-34

This chapter is a repetition of 2 Kings 24:18 – 25:30. It was probably added to emphasize the fact that Jeremiah's prophecies had been fulfilled. Jerusalem was besieged by Babylon for one year and a half. **52:4-6** The book closes with Jehoiachin's release by Nebuchadnezzar's successor in 561 BC. His release after 37 years may have given hope to the other exiles. **52:31** God has spoken!

Review Questions on Lesson 12
Jeremiah 47 – 52

1. When Nebuchadnezzar invaded the **Philistines**, the men
   would flee and leave their _____ behind.
   47:3

2. The **Moabites** were descendants of _____.
   They worshiped _____ as their god. 48:13
   They were known for their _____. 48:29

3. The **Ammonites** were descendants of _____.
   Their worship of _____ involved _____
   sacrifices. 49:1

4. The Edomites, descendants of _____, rejoiced over
   the destruction of _____. (Obadiah 10-14)
   Edom would _____ the cup of God's wrath. 49:12

5. God said, "I will kindle a _____ in the wall of
   Damascus," the capital of _____.

6. **Kedar** was related to _____ and was a
   nomadic _____ nation. Who would strike
   Kedar and the kingdoms of Hazor? 49:28-33

   _____

7. The LORD said, "I will break the _____ of **Elam**,"
   and "I will set My _____ in Elam." 49:35, 38

8. _____ the Persian overthrew the Medes who
   controlled Elam and established the Persian Empire,
   replacing the Babylonian Empire. He would become
   God's instrument over other nations.

9. The Elamites heard the _____ on Pentecost.

10. What is to happen to **Babylon**? 50:1-5

    _____

11. After Babylon's fall, the people of Israel and of Judah
    will come together and seek _____ _____, and they
    will ask for the way to _____, saying, "Let us join
    ourselves to the _____ in a perpetual, everlasting
    _____that will not be _____." 50:4-5

12. The LORD of hosts, the God of Israel, says,
    "Behold, I will punish the king of _____ and his
    land, as I have punished the king of _____. And
    I will bring _____ again to his habitation. 50:18-19

13. Babylon had been _____against the LORD. 50:29

14. The LORD has the right to judge the nations because he
    has made the earth by his _____; established the
    world by his _____ and stretched out the heavens
    by his _____. 51:15

15. Babylon (and Persia) were God's _____ _____
    against sinful nations. (51:20)

16. Who read the scroll containing the judgment against
    Babylon and then threw it into the Euphrates River
    as a symbolic act? 51:61 _____

17. How long was Jerusalem besieged by the army
    of Babylon? 52:4-8 _____

18. After _____ years of captivity, Jehoiachin
    (former king of Judah) was brought out of prison by
    _____ king of Babylon, and he ate bread
    before _____ _____ all the days of his life. 52:31-34

Lesson 13

Lamentations
Over The Fall of Jerusalem

Jewish and Christian writers agree that Jeremiah wrote this book soon after the destruction of Jerusalem in 586 BC. The Septuagint (a Greek translation of the Old Testament) calls the book, "Lamentations of Jeremiah." Jeremiah was an eyewitness of the siege and destruction of Jerusalem. The siege lasted one and a half years.

Lamentations is a funeral song of grief describing the suffering and sorrow at the passing of the glorious city of Jerusalem to rubble. Each chapter is a poem.

Chapter 1 – Jerusalem, a Lonely Weeping Widow
Chapter 2 – God's Anger over Jerusalem
Chapter 3 – Hope during Affliction
Chapter 4 – The Sufferings of the Siege
Chapter 5 – A Prayer for Restoration

In the midst of sorrow and despair, Jeremiah's faith gives him hope: *"The LORD is my portion, says my soul; therefore, I will hope in him."* (3:24)

There are three themes: (1) mourning over Jerusalem's sufferings and destruction, (2) the confession of sins, and (3) the hope of restoration in the future.

Jerusalem, a Lonely Weeping Widow
Lamentations 1

How lonely sits the city that was full of people! How like a widow is she, who was great among the nations! **1:1** NKJV She weeps bitterly because none of her lovers will comfort her. All of her friends had become her enemies. **1:2** The LORD has afflicted her because of the multitude of her sins. **1:5**

Judah has gone into captivity. She dwells among the nations. The roads to Zion mourn because no one comes to the set feasts. **1:3, 4** ᴺᴷᴶⱽ *In the days of her affliction and roaming, Jerusalem remembers all her pleasant things.* **1:7** ᴺᴷᴶⱽ "By the rivers of Babylon, there we sat down, yea, we wept, when we remembered Zion." (Psalm 137:1) In good times, we tend to forget that God is the one who is giving us the blessings we are enjoying; we may take them for granted. "Every good gift and every perfect gift is from above, and comes down from the Father." (James 1:17)

Jerusalem has grievously sinned; therefore, she is removed. **1:8** Those who had honored the city now despise her. *She did not consider her destiny; therefore, her collapse was awesome.* **1:9** ᴺᴷᴶⱽ Sinners who are not seeking God are not considering their destiny. "There is a way that seems right to a man, but its end is the way of death." (Proverbs 14:12) A sinful nation is not considering its destiny. "Righteousness exalts a nation. But sin is a disgrace to any people." ᴺᴵⱽ (Proverbs 14:34)

Jerusalem asks, *"Is it nothing to you, all you that pass by? Behold, and see if there is any sorrow like unto my sorrow, which is done to me, wherewith the LORD has afflicted me ... He has sent fire into my bones."* **1:12-13** *"The LORD has trodden the virgin, the daughter of Judah as in a winepress. For these things I weep."* **1:15, 16** She confesses, *"The LORD is righteous, for I rebelled against his commandment ... I called for my lovers, but they deceived me."* **1:18, 19** She pleads, *"Behold, O LORD, for I am in distress ... my heart is turned within me, for I have grievously rebelled."* **1:20** She closes her lament with a prayer that her enemies may be punished for all their wickedness. *"All my enemies have heard of my trouble; they are glad. ... Let all their wickedness come before you; and do unto them as you have done unto me for all my transgressions, for my sighs are many and my heart is faint."* **1:21-22**

God's Anger over Jerusalem
Lamentations 2

How has the Lord covered the daughter of Zion with a cloud in his anger and cast down from heaven unto earth the beauty of Israel, and remembered not his footstool in the day of his anger! **2:1** Jerusalem was "the daughter of Zion," and the temple of God was "the beauty of Israel." The Ark of the Covenant is "the footstool of our God." (1 Chron. 28:2)

In fierce anger He has cut off all the strength of Israel. **2:3** ᴺᴬˢᴮ The "horn of Israel" refers to its power. *"The Lord was as an enemy. He has swallowed up Israel. He has swallowed up her palaces. He has destroyed his strongholds ... He has violently taken away his tabernacle* (his temple) *... The LORD has caused the solemn feasts and sabbaths to be forgotten in Zion and has despised in the indignation of his anger the king and the priest."* **2:5-6**

Jeremiah says, *"My eyes fail from weeping ... because children and infants faint in the streets of the city. They say to their mothers, 'Where is bread?' as their lives ebb away in their mother's arms."* **2:11-12** ᴺᴵⱽ Jeremiah gives a cause for their suffering, *"Your prophets have seen for you false and deceptive visions."* **2:14** ᴺᴷᴶⱽ They had listened to these false prophets who had failed to rebuke their sins. **12:15-16**

"The LORD has done that which he had devised; he has fulfilled his word that he commanded in days of old." **2:17** Moses had predicted that all these terrors would come upon them if they broke God's covenant, including starvation that would cause women to eat their own children. (Lev. 26:27-45) *"Look, O LORD, and consider: ... Should women eat their offspring, the children they have cared for? Young and old lie together in the dust of the streets; my young men and maidens have fallen by the sword ... in the day of your anger."* **2:20-21** ᴺᴵⱽ

Hope during Affliction
Lamentation 3

I am the man who has seen affliction under the rod of his wrath; he has driven and brought me into darkness without any light. **3:1-2** ᴱˢⱽ Jeremiah had suffered God's wrath with his people. He does not understand why God's judgment on his nation is so severe.

He has made my flesh and my skin waste away; he has broken my bones; he has besieged and enveloped me with bitterness and tribulation. **3:4-5** ᴱˢⱽ Jeremiah describes in figurative language how he felt during the siege. He looked and felt like an old man due to his weakened physical condition. The prophet was personally feeling the effects of the siege; he felt shut in.

Though I call and cry for help, he shuts out my prayers. **3:8** ᴱˢⱽ His prayers for deliverance from the siege would not be heard. God had said to him in Jeremiah 11:14, "Do not pray for this people, or lift up a cry or prayer for them; for I will not hear them in the time that they cry out to me because of their trouble." ᴺᴷᴶⱽ *He has made me desolate.* **3:11** Jeremiah feels that he is the target of God's arrows. **3:12** (cf. Job 7:20; 16:12)

I have become the laughingstock of all peoples; the object of their taunts all day long. **3:14** ᴱˢⱽ He was mocked when he tried to warn his people of this calamity, and now they are blaming him for it.

He has filled me with bitterness ... my soul is bereft of peace; I have forgotten what happiness is, so I say, "My endurance has perished; so has my hope from the LORD." **3:15, 17-18** ᴱˢⱽ He calls upon God to remember his affliction. **3:19** Just as he is about to give up, Jeremiah remembers those things that gave him hope: *But this I recall to mind, and therefore I have hope.* **3:21** ᴱˢⱽ

The steadfast love of the LORD never ceases; his mercies never come to an end; they are new every morning; great is your faithfulness. **3:22-23** ^{ESV} Jeremiah realizes that he and others are still alive because of God's mercies. His compassions for us may be seen every day. Just as the Lord provided fresh new manna every morning for Israel in the wilderness, he provides those things that we need each day. (Matthew 6:31-34) His faithfulness is great. Jeremiah stated, *"The LORD is my portion," says my soul, "therefore I will hope in him."* **3:24** ^{ESV} Fanny J. Crosby expresses the same thoughts in her hymn, "Thou My Everlasting Portion". Wayne Jackson made this application: "The Lord is all we need; our hope is anchored in him." [43]

The LORD is good to those who wait for him, to the soul who seeks him. It is good that one should wait quietly for the salvation of the LORD ... For the LORD will not cast off forever, but though he causes grief, he will have compassion according to the multitude of his mercies. **3:25-26, 31-32** ^{ESV}

Why should a living man complain, a man about the punishment of his sins? Let us test and examine our ways, and return to the LORD! **3:39-40** ^{ESV}

I called on your name, O LORD, from the depths of the pit; you heard my plea: "Do not close your ear to my cry for help!" You came near when I called on you; you said, "Do not fear!" **3:55-57** ^{ESV} This may be a reference to the time when Jeremiah was delivered from the dungeon, a muddy waterless cistern. (Jeremiah 38:6-13) This should have given hope to the Jews during their exile.

O LORD, you have pleaded the case for my soul; you have redeemed my life. **3:58** ^{NKJV} God was an advocate for Jermiah - his defense attorney. And "we have an Advocate with the father, Jesus Christ the righteous." (1 John 2:1)

---

[43] Wayne Jackson, *Jeremiah & Lamentations*, p. 158

The Sufferings of the Siege
Lamentations 4

How the gold has lost its luster, the fine gold has become dull! The sacred gems are scattered at the head of every street. How precious the sons of Zion, once considered their weight in gold, are considered as pots of clay, the work of a potter's hands! **4:1-2** ^{NIV}

The horrible conditions during the siege of Jerusalem are described. The inhabitants of the once glorious city of God are compared to fine gold that has lost its luster. The people are now like pots of clay.

Because of thirst the infant's tongue sticks to the roof of its mouth; the children beg for bread, but no one gives it to them. Those who once ate delicacies are destitute in the streets. Those nurtured in purple now lie on ash heaps. The punishment of my people is greater than Sodom, which was overthrown in a moment without a hand turned to help. **4:4-6** ^{NIV} The siege lasted for one and a half years. Children were starving to death. Those who once ate expensive food were destitute having nothing to eat. The punishment of Jerusalem therefore was greater than the punishment of Sodom, which was quickly destroyed. Those who once were fair in appearance are now *blacker than coal,* and *they are not known in the streets* because *their skin cleaves to their bones.* **4:7-8** *Those slain by the sword are better off than those who die of hunger.* **4:9** ^{NKJV} *Compassionate women boiled their own children; they became food for them because of the destruction.* **4:10** ^{NASB}

The LORD has accomplished fury; he has poured out his fierce anger, and has kindled a fire in Zion. ... For the sins of her prophets and the iniquities of her priests ... the anger of the LORD has divided them; he will no more regard them. **4:11, 13, 16**

The Edomites rejoiced over the fall of Jerusalem (Psalm 137:7), but their time of punishment was coming. However, Jerusalem's punishment would end. **4:21-22**

A Prayer for Restoration
Lamentations 5

"Remember, O LORD, what has come upon us; consider and behold our reproach." **5:1** Their inheritance and homes had been turned over to foreigners. They had become like fatherless orphans, and their mothers like widows. **5:2-3** Water and bread were scarce. **5:4-9** Their skin was "hot as an oven" with the fever of diseases caused by famine. **5:10** NKJV Women were raped by the Babylonian soldiers. **5:11** Their noble men were tortured, and their elders disrespected. **5:12** Their young men and boys were given hard labor. **5:13** The elders were no longer at the gate of the city; the music of the young men was not heard any more. **5:14** Their joy had turned to mourning. **5:15**

They said, *"The crown has fallen from our head. Woe to us, for we have sinned."* **5:16** NKJV *"You, O LORD, remain forever; thy throne from generation to generation."* **5:19**

Then they prayed, *"Turn us back to You, O LORD, and we shall be restored; renew our days as of old, unless You have utterly rejected us, and are very angry with us!"* **5:21-22** NKJV They needed God's grace and mercy.

Review Questions on Lesson 13

1. Jeremiah wrote Lamentations in _____ BC shortly after the destruction of the city of _____.

2. There are _____ funeral poems for Jerusalem in the book of Lamentations.

3. The three themes in Lamentations are
   (1) _____,
   (2) _____,
   (3) _____.

4. Jerusalem was like a lonely weeping _____. 1:1-2

5. "The roads of Zion mourn because no one comes to her set _____." 1:4

6. The LORD has afflicted her because of her _____. 1:5

7. Judah did not consider her _____. 1:9

8. Chapter 2, God's _____ is over Jerusalem.

9. "The daughter of Zion" refers to _____.
   2:1

10. "The beauty of Israel" refers to the _____. 2:1

11. "His footstool" is the _____ of the _____. 2:1

12. The destruction of the _____ is described in 2:6-7.

13. Most of the prophets had seen _____ and _____ visions. 2:14

14. Young children _____ from _____. 2:11,19

15. "Should women _____ their offspring?" 2:20

16. "The day of the LORD's _____" describes the destruction of Jerusalem. (2:21)

17. Chapter three is about "_____ in the Lord during _____."

18. "I am the man that has seen _____ by the rod of his wrath." 3:1

19. "He has filled me with _____." 3:15
    "I have forgotten what _____ is." 3:17 ESV

20. "This I recall to my mind, therefore I have _____ ...
    The LORD is my _____, says my soul,
    therefore I will _____ in him." 3:21, 24 ESV

21. "The LORD is good unto them that _____ for him,
    to the soul that _____ him." 3:25

22. Chapter four is about "The _____ of the Siege".

23. Their infants and young children were without _____
    and _____. 4:4

24. "Those slain by the sword are better off than those who
    die of _____." 4:9

25. The LORD "kindled a fire in Zion" because of the sins of
    her _____ and of her _____. 4:11-13

26. Chapter five is "A Prayer for _____".
    "Turn us back to _____, O LORD, and we shall be
    _____." 5:21